MEN OF STEEL

Qui Nguyen

D0556722

BROADWAY PLAY PUBLISHING INC
224 E 62nd St, NY, NY 10065
www.broadwayplaypub.com
info@broadwayplaypub.com

MEN OF STEEL
© Copyright 2007 by Qui Nguyen

First printing: August 2007
This printing: October 2015
I S B N: 978-0-88145-347-8

Book design: Marie Donovan
Word processing: Microsoft Word
Typographic controls: Ventura Publisher
Typeface: Palatino
Printed and bound in the U S A

MEN OF STEEL was originally produced by Vampire Cowboys Theatre Company from 15 March-8 April 2007 at Center Stage, NY, with the following cast and credits:

BURNOUT, LUKAS, DADDY . . . . Noshir Dalal
HELEN HARPER, MELINDA . . . . Sharon Eisman
JASON PRICE A K A CAPTAIN JUSTICE . . Jason Liebman
HURT, ANDERSON, BRYANT . . . . Tom Myers
LIBERTY LADY, CAMILLE, MOMMY . . . Melissa Paladino
ANDY A K A THE HOODED MENACE,
   KING, JOE DICKENS, WARDEN . . . . Jeremy Sarver
THE MOLE, DAMON, CHRISTIAN . . . . Paco Tolson
MALCOLM A K A MAELSTROM,
   MARCUS, REYNOLDS . . . . Temar Underwood

Director . . . . Robert Ross Parker
Producer . . . . Abby Marcus
Fight Director . . . . Marius Hanford
Scenic/Lighting Designer . . . . Nick Francone
Costume Designer . . . . Jessica Wegener
Sound Designer . . . . Patrick Shearer
Weapon Design/Construction . . . . Nathan Lemoine
Graphic Artist . . . . Chris Brown
A S Ms . . . . Florencio Palomo & Sharon Walsh
Publicity/Press Rep . . . . Jim Baldassare

PROLOGUE:
JUSTICE PART ONE

(In the darkness we hear the chaotic sounds of police sirens and helicopters rushing to a crime scene.)

(Projection: A comic book image of CAPTAIN JUSTICE *holding the dead body of a girl)*

(Projection: "(The name of the producing company)")

(Projection: A comic book image of two thugs running in an alleyway.)

(Projection: "presents")

(Projection: A comic book image of CAPTAIN JUSTICE's *shadow standing in the alleyway)*

(Projection: "MEN OF STEEL")

(Projection: A close-up image of the eyes of a very angry CAPTAIN JUSTICE)

(Projection: "A Vampire Cowboy Creation")

(Projection: A comic book image of CAPTAIN JUSTICE *covered in blood.)*

(Lights rise on the real-life CAPTAIN JUSTICE. *He stands alone silently in the exact position as the comic book images.)*

OFFICER: *(O S)* Captain Justice, you are hereby under arrest for the murder of Thomas Hurt and Bernie Dalton. We have been given the authority to use lethal

force in this matter. You are surrounded. We ask that
you stand down.

(LIBERTY LADY, *a female superhero dressed as brightly and
patriotic as* CAPTAIN JUSTICE *enters.*)

(*She stands staring at her former mentor.*)

(CAPTAIN JUSTICE *looks over to* LIBERTY LADY.)

LIBERTY LADY: Please, Cap, don't make me do this.

(CAPTAIN JUSTICE *throws down his shield and begins to
leave, but suddenly turns and attacks* LIBERTY LADY.)

(*They fight brutally and hard, but in the end,* LIBERTY LADY
stands victorious.)

LIBERTY LADY: (*Into a walkie-talkie*) The Captain's down.
Repeat: The Captain's down. Send in reinforcements.

(*Black out*)

SCENE I

(*Projection: "Chapter One: Maelstrom"*)

(*Projection: "Chicago, Illinois."*)

(*Lights up on* MAELSTROM)

MAELSTROM: A single bullet. A simple archaic piece
of metal no bigger than a human tear drop. So small it
would disappear on a table full of photos—memories—
random useless trinkets that signify nothing. So small,
yet it can tear through flesh—destroy a life—rip a
soul from this existence and send it hurdling towards
oblivion. A bullet—insignificant in its size, but almost
Godlike in its power.

   How did we get here? Rewind twenty four hours.

(*Lights come up on* BURNOUT *holding a knife against*
HELEN HARPER's *throat.* HURT *stands watching guard.*)

BURNOUT: You smell like vanilla. I love vanilla—vanilla cupcakes, vanilla ice cream, vanilla fish—

HELEN: Vanilla fish?

BURNOUT: It's an acquired taste.

HURT: Yo, Burnout! We're clear—ain't a soul out here anywhere. We gots what they call unadulterated privacy.

BURNOUT: Do you hear that? Do you? Now do you now realize the gravity of this situation?

HURT: Oh, man, she's pretty.

BURNOUT: Yes, she is.

HURT: She looks like my mom.

(Both BURNOUT and HELEN look at HURT.)

HURT: I mean...your mom?
My sister?

BURNOUT: Just keep an eye out for trouble, will ya? We're gonna have some fun with this one.

(As BURNOUT grabs HELEN, MAELSTROM enters the scene.)

HURT: Uh, Burnout...
Burnout!

BURNOUT: What?

HURT: Eye spy trouble.

(BURNOUT turns and sees MAELSTROM.)

BURNOUT: Shit!

HELEN: About fucking time.

(BURNOUT quickly grabs HELEN and places his knife next to her throat.)

BURNOUT: Yo, man, I will friggin' cut this bitch. I will. Back off.

HURT: Guys, thanks for all the attention. It was really flattering, but it's time to roll the credit sequence.

(*Suddenly,* HELEN *takes out her two assailants.*)

HELEN: How ya doing, Mal? Creepy as ever, I see.

MAELSTROM: What are you doing in my city, Helen?

HELEN: Why so terse, Detective? Got no time to chit-chat?

MAELSTROM: A stunt like this could've gotten you hurt.

HELEN: By these two pussies? Please. You're forgetting who you're talking to.

MAELSTROM: Was this all to get my attention?

HELEN: Sorry, it's not like I have your cell-phone number.

MAELSTROM: What is it you want?

HELEN: What would any girl want from a tall, dark, and brooding man in black? I want your help.

MAELSTROM: I don't do requests.

HELEN: I'm not asking—I'm telling. There's a Benedict amongst you boys and he's made the make on my husband. He's figured out Cap's identity which means he's coming after me, you, everyone we know. So I figure I can either sit around and wait for the hit or I can go hunting and catch me a killer. I'm choosing the latter and I'm here looking for some back. That's you.

MAELSTROM: Why don't you get your husband to do the job?

HELEN: I don't need a superhero. What I need is a detective. The gossip lines say you're the world's greatest. This little girl is hoping the talk is true.

MAELSTROM: You know your hubby and I don't get along. I don't think he'd appreciate us making time.

HELEN: He's not here—even if he were, I'm no Doris Day. I make my own calls.

MAELSTROM: One question.

HELEN: Make it sexy.

MAELSTROM: What's in it for me?

(HELEN *pulls out a gun and points it at* MAELSTROM's *face.*)

HELEN: I don't shoot you in your fucking face.

MAELSTROM: *(Approvingly)* Nice.

(Lights close tightly onto MAELSTROM.*)*

MAELSTROM: For you to understand the high stakes of this poker game, you gotta know what's been anted up. Supers—once regular citizens—once, everyday sheep living their everyday sheep lives—once, normal, until Uncle Sam recruited and reshaped their molecular structure.

I'm not one of them—make no mistake, minus the mask, I'm as mortal as any of you.

My name is Maelstrom and this is my city.

Every hero has a story. Some are chosen—some are made. This is the diametrically opposed chasm between him and myself. He was Sam's banner boy—the skinny soldier they recreated into America's ultimate icon. I was the self-created other. I tell you this so you can know—so you can understand why this had to be done.

In the beginning...

(Crossfade to two teenagers, ANDY *and* JASON. ANDY *threatening* JASON*)*

ANDY: Hey, look at the little sissy boy! Where's your boyfriend, sissy-boy?

JASON: Give me back my bag!

ANDY: Is his rich ass too good to come to school? Is that it? Left you here all by your lonesome?

JASON: I'm not scared of you.

ANDY: You're not, are ya? Boo.

JASON: Stop it!

ANDY: Or what? You're gonna tell on me? Is that it?
You're gonna rat me out? Oh man, you are a full-on
gay-wad, ain't ya?

(MAELSTROM *enters.*)

MAELSTROM: Leave him alone, Andy.

ANDY: *(To* JASON*)* Just when we're having fun...
    What's up, rich boy?

MAELSTROM: I told you, Andy, the kid's off limits.
He's under my wing.

ANDY: No need to get your brow furrowed, rich boy.
I'm just playing with your friend here. We're just
fucking around. Ain't that right, Jay?

MAELSTROM: Get your hands off of him.

ANDY: And if I don't?

(ANDY *and* MAELSTROM *stare the other down.*)

ANDY: I'll see you after school. You and me—we gonna
have some fun. See ya when the last bell rings. *(He exits.)*

JASON: Thanks, Mal.

MAELSTROM: You okay?

JASON: I think he ripped my shirt.

MAELSTROM: What'd you do to him?

JASON: I didn't do anything.

MAELSTROM: Andy doesn't go wolf-man unless
someone steps on his tail. What's the story?

(Beat)

JASON: I wouldn't give him the sneak.

MAELSTROM: Which class?

JASON: Algebra.

MAELSTROM: Jason—

JASON: It's wrong, Mal. I'm not going to support cheating. What would that make me if I got behind somethin' like that?

MAELSTROM: Ask that to your shirt.

JASON: What are you doing here today?

MAELSTROM: It's school. It happens five times a week with the exception of major holidays and summer break.

JASON: I'm aware of the schedule, Mal, I'm just saying—

MAELSTROM: Well, I hate to inform you, I'm not some Doogie Howser that's excluded from the rigors of public education. I'm stuck in this hole just like anyone else.

JASON: Trust me, no one's calling you Doogie. I just thought you'd take today off. You know because of...

MAELSTROM: My father?

JASON: Well, yeah...

MAELSTROM: You should be happy I decided to show. If I didn't, Andy would have royally kicked your hide.

JASON: I could have handled myself.

MAELSTROM: Right.

JASON: I coulda.

MAELSTROM: Jason, there's freshmen girls in this hole that pack a meaner punch.

JASON: I'm working out.

MAELSTROM: And it shows.

JASON: Do they got any leads?

MAELSTROM: No.

JASON: They'll catch them, Mal. I know they will.

MAELSTROM: I wish I were as hopeful.

JASON: They will.

MAELSTROM: But hope is only good for prisoners and bums playing the lotto. Unfortunately, I'm neither.

JASON: Chicago has a great police department. I'm sure they have the best men on the job. They'll catch them.

(Silence)

MAELSTROM: Jason, have you ever hated anyone?

JASON: What?

MAELSTROM: Have you ever hated anyone?

JASON: I'm not too fond of Andy.

MAELSTROM: I'm not talking about this schoolyard crap—I'm talking hate—real hate—the kind that boils up deep—wholly consumes—feeds on you until you're nothin' but a husk?
    Because I hate. I hate someone I have never met. There is someone or someones in this world that I despise beyond anything in all of creation and I have no idea who they are. Do you know what that's like? Can you even imagine? I want to find them and break them, Jason—like they broke me—like how they broke my father.

JASON: Golly. I don't think I'm capable of that.

MAELSTROM: For your sake, I hope you're right.

JASON: Thanks for getting my backpack, Mal. *(He exits.)*

MAELSTROM: We're in a profession of keeping secrets. Our identities, our loved ones, our drinking buddies— these are our Achilles heels—these are the walking/ talking weaknesses that can topple even an indestructible man. That's why Helen Harper is so worried. She knows perhaps better than any of us that the only way to beat someone who is unbreakable is to get him by the heart. Unlike any of his enemies, she's the only one who has ever brought Captain Justice to his knees. She's his Delilah. We all have our weaknesses. Some not as obvious as others.

(ANDY *enters and puts his hand on* MAELSTROM'S *shoulder.*)

(*Suddenly,* ANDY *and* MAELSTROM *fall into a very rough, but sensual kiss.*)

(*Fade to...*)

(*Lights up on* LIBERTY LADY *and* HELEN *at the doorway of the Justice Lab.*)

LIBERTY LADY: I don't know how many times I've told ya, Helen—you can't just traipse into the Justice Lab any time you want! Ever thought about maybe using the phone first?

HELEN: Ever thought about wearing a shirt that fits?

LIBERTY LADY: Stay out.

HELEN: Where's my husband?

LIBERTY LADY: You don't think I won't just pick you up and throw your ass out? You do know I have superpowers, right?

HELEN: Being a whore is a superpower?

LIBERTY LADY: Wow. You are a hoot!

HELEN: Where is he?

LIBERTY LADY: Overseas quelling a conflict.

HELEN: I need to get him word.

LIBERTY LADY: What? Do you need pookie to pick up some midol on his way home from work because you're a raging bitch today?

HELEN: Someone's made the make.

LIBERTY LADY: What?

HELEN: We're in trouble.

LIBERTY LADY: You speaking serious?

HELEN: How many of the Honor Guard knows Cap's alias besides yourself?

LIBERTY LADY: That's it. End of story. We don't share that kinda intel.

HELEN: Then explain this.

(HELEN *hands* LIBERTY LADY *the note.*)

LIBERTY LADY: "Tell your hubby to stop sailing or we're knocking on your door. The Captain has twenty-four to get land-locked."
   This came to you?

HELEN: It was on my desk at the Daily Ledger. Who else knows besides yourself.

LIBERTY LADY: No one. Cept Maelstrom in Chicago who went A-WOL, but he ain't gonna breathe a peep. He's too tied—giving up Cap would undress himself.

HELEN: That's it?

LIBERTY LADY: That's it.

HELEN: Any bad guys?

LIBERTY LADY: There's rumor that the Hooded Menace may know, but he's locked up deep. Steel City deep. Ain't word coming from his yapper.

HELEN: I need you to call him home, Liberty. Pronto.

LIBERTY LADY: Let's go.

(*Fade to...*)

MAELSTROM: Weaknesses. We all have weaknesses.

JASON: *(O S)* BUMRUSH!

(JASON *storms in and tackles* MAELSTROM. ANDY *fades into the background.*)

(*The two boys wrestle.* MAELSTROM *takes the advantage and puts* JASON *in a headlock.*)

MAELSTROM: Please tell me this is not what you call fighting.

JASON: I'm just about to do my big reverse move.

MAELSTROM: You're clearly losing.

JASON: Maybe this is part of my brilliant strategy.

MAELSTROM: Bleeding is part of your brilliant strategy?

JASON: Perhaps.

MAELSTROM: Don't take this the wrong way, friend, but the military is going to kill you dead.

JASON: You promised you weren't going to give me shit.

MAELSTROM: Who's giving you shit? I'm just pointing out a fact. Fact: you fight like a big ol' Golden Girl—and I'm not referring to the strangely man-ish Bea Arthur.

JASON: Then why don't you enlist too? Keep me outta trouble.

MAELSTROM: I told you. That's not gonna happen.

JASON: SWEET CHIN MUSIC!

(*Abruptly,* JASON *goes for a mule kick on* MAELSTROM. MAELSTROM *counters and drops him on his ass.*)

MAELSTROM: Look, friend, first rule of entrapment is not to announce your moves.

JASON: This is what I'm talking about, Mal. You already got this stuff down. Why don't you just come with me? Use that cranium for good.

MAELSTROM: I don't think so.

JASON: Why not, Mal? It's not like you're doing
anything here...ya know, besides being rich.
The money has to get boring at some point. Right?
Okay, maybe not, but you'll be with your bro.
Come on, Yoko, don't break up the band. Look, don't
you want to do something worthwhile with your life?

MAELSTROM: It's not that.

JASON: Then spill.

MAELSTROM: I just don't agree with it, okay? The world
doesn't need more soldiers.

JASON: What? You really think that?

MAELSTROM: Look at this city, Jason—our home—
it needs help. It's getting overrun by the worst kind
of element. How can I worry about folks overseas
when they're folks over here dying in places like
Cabrini Green. It's not that I don't want to help—
it's just this place, this city—it could use a little help too.

JASON: And you're gonna do that?

MAELSTROM: Maybe I got a plan.

JASON: Bagging young ladies ain't exactly community
service.

MAELSTROM: I'm talking serious. This town is my
future, Jason. I can't go with you. I'm sorry.

JASON: Don't be. They don't let in pussies anyhow.

(*The two boys hug.*)

(JASON *exits.*)

MAELSTROM: A bullet's path is not a straight line.
Measure it's arch and trajectory, you'll see that it
actually falls. From a long enough distance, you can
see it drop. The bullet that stole my father's life finally
ended up dropping on me. The bullet that's now aimed
at Helen has a different destination altogether.

(HELEN enters.)

HELEN: Mal? Malcolm. I'm here.

MAELSTROM: Did you get word to Jason?

HELEN: The message is sent.

MAELSTROM: Does she know anything?

HELEN: Only names she put in play was you and Menace. Menace is out considering he's locked up in Steel. And you...

MAELSTROM: What about me?

HELEN: No, that's crazy.

MAELSTROM: What makes you figure I'm not the Benedict?

HELEN: Jason once said that if the shit ever hit the fan, you'd be the one he'd want at his back.

MAELSTROM: He said that? Smart man.

HELEN: So what do we do now?

MAELSTROM: Lay low. Wait til your hubby gets home.

HELEN: I don't play that game.

MAELSTROM: The goal is to get Jason back here where he belongs, not thrust you in the middle of a fire-fight.

HELEN: I'm not looking for action, but I'm no damsel in distress. Must I remind you—I'm an investigative reporter by trade, I've taken down my share of low-life just as much as you.

MAELSTROM: This is different.

HELEN: The only thing different is this time the story is me. I want to get this joker. I want to see him hung to dry.

MAELSTROM: You want to keep hunting? It could get dangerous.

HELEN: I just want to do my part.

MAELSTROM: Then come with me. I need to show you something.

(*Fade to...*)

MAELSTROM: The problem with being a super is after doing it long enough, you begin to believe you actually are invulnerable. Just because a bullet can't pierce your skin doesn't mean you can't die. I remember the first time I ever saw him in his uniform. It was during my year one—the first days in my war against crime. We were different men all those years ago—Jason still fought for Americans and I still battled villains as silly as his costume. We were still idealists.

(*Enter* THE MOLE.)

THE MOLE: You'll never stop me, Maelstrom! I'm too crafty, too ingenious, too clever to ever be beaten. I am the human personification of the word "genius". I am THE MOLE, the most astute criminal mind since—

(MAELSTROM *punches* THE MOLE *right in the face, knocking him out.*)

MAELSTROM: You talk too goddamn much. Dumbass.

(CAPTAIN JUSTICE *enters.*)

CAPTAIN JUSTICE: Stand back, Citizen. Captain Justice is here!

MAELSTROM: What in the blue hell are you wearing?

CAPTAIN JUSTICE: Malcolm Wallace. So this is what you did with all your money, huh? Turned yourself into a what? A vampire detective? I like the name—Maelstrom. Malcolm. It's nifty.

MAELSTROM: Jason Price.

Malcolm = Maelstrom = Batman.
Jason = Captain Justice = Cap. America

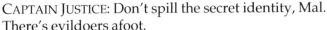

CAPTAIN JUSTICE: Don't spill the secret identity, Mal. There's evildoers afoot.

MAELSTROM: Your costume's kinda gay.

CAPTAIN JUSTICE: Fuck you. This shit's hot.

MAELSTROM: If you were riding a float.

CAPTAIN JUSTICE: Isn't this cool, man? We're both superheroes! What powers you got? Check it— I got strength, speed, invulnerability. And if I concentrate real hard, I can almost guess the future.

MAELSTROM: Bullshit.

CAPTAIN JUSTICE: I knew you were going to say that.

MAELSTROM: Fuck off.

CAPTAIN JUSTICE: Saw that coming a mile away.

MAELSTROM: Did they mean to write fag on your uniform like that?

CAPTAIN JUSTICE: They didn't write fag on my uniform.

MAELSTROM: Seriously, it's right there.

(MAELSTROM *points at* CAPTAIN JUSTICE'*s chest. When* CAPTAIN JUSTICE *looks,* MAELSTROM *flicks him in the nose.)*

MAELSTROM: Yeah, you're quite the psychic.

CAPTAIN JUSTICE: So what can you do? Power-wise. What's your thing?

MAELSTROM: I have gadgets.

CAPTAIN JUSTICE: And...

MAELSTROM: That's it—I have gadgets.

CAPTAIN JUSTICE: That's it?

MAELSTROM: And a boomerang?

CAPTAIN JUSTICE: Dude—

MAELSTROM: Fuck you—I'm scary.

CAPTAIN JUSTICE: Uh-huh.

MAELSTROM: Listen to this.

(MAELSTROM *suddenly grabs* CAPTAIN JUSTICE *by his shirt and pulls him close.*)

MAELSTROM: *(Like Michael Keaton's Batman)* I'm Maelstrom.

(CAPTAIN JUSTICE *slowly forms a laugh.*)

MAELSTROM: So what are you doing back in my town?

CAPTAIN JUSTICE: Uncle Sam sent me. They heard about what you were doing out here in Chi-town and wanted me to make sure you were on the up and up.

MAELSTROM: And am I?

(Suddenly, THE MOLE *jumps to his feet.)*

THE MOLE: You think I'd be so easily defeated? You thought wrong, Maelstrom! I have the equivalent strength and skill of a MOLE! If you try to take me down, I'll just bury you!

CAPTAIN JUSTICE: *(To* MAELSTROM*)* Let me.

MAELSTROM: Go ahead.

THE MOLE: Who are you?

CAPTAIN JUSTICE: JUSTICE PUNCH!

(CAPTAIN JUSTICE *takes a wild swing at* THE MOLE. THE MOLE *dodges and throws* CAPTAIN JUSTICE *to the ground.*)

THE MOLE: Ha-ha, Justice Punch! You're no match for me, for I will not go down so easily!

(MAELSTROM *strolls up and stun-guns him.*)

MAELSTROM: See—gadgets. Superpowers still don't make up for smarts.

CAPTAIN JUSTICE: Yeah, I gotcha. But I'm going to get good at this—you'll see.

MAELSTROM: Not if someone kills you first, Jay.

CAPTAIN JUSTICE: Stop calling me Jason!

MAELSTROM: Sorry...Captain.

CAPTAIN JUSTICE: Look, Mal, I actually came here to talk to you about something.

MAELSTROM: What?

CAPTAIN JUSTICE: It's about our past.

MAELSTROM: What tree you barking up?

CAPTAIN JUSTICE: You know when we were kids—hanging out, screwing around?

MAELSTROM: Yeah.

CAPTAIN JUSTICE: We were always close, right? Best friends.

MAELSTROM: Yeah.

CAPTAIN JUSTICE: Well, there's something I need to tell you. Do you remember that kid Andy who used to beat me up all the time?

MAELSTROM: How could I forget?

CAPTAIN JUSTICE: Well, there's something I found out about him. Something ripe. Disgusting. The thing is...well, he's...he's—

MAELSTROM: Gay?

CAPTAIN JUSTICE: What!?! He's gay? I didn't know that. Holy crap!

MAELSTROM: Oh, I don't know! I was just guessing.

CAPTAIN JUSTICE: Oh. Alright.
   No, he's turned to a life of crime. He's the Hooded Menace. My arch-nemesis.

MAELSTROM: What?

CAPTAIN JUSTICE: I thought we could go take him down together. That's why I'm here. I want to do a team-up.

(THE MOLE *pops back up.*)

THE MOLE: Alright, assholes! You think you can just whack THE MOLE and not feel some retribution? You are incorrect, for what you don't about know THE MOLE is that he has—

(CAPTAIN JUSTICE *and* MAELSTROM *step up.*)

THE MOLE: Okay, seriously now, let me finish what I'm saying before you get all hit-ty. Alright? Just stand there for one second, please—hold the violence. What I was going to say was—I have a seismic earthquake-inator!
    You weren't expecting that now, were you? Ha-ha-ha!

(THE MOLE *activates the device knocking* CAPTAIN JUSTICE *and* MAELSTROM *on their asses.*)

(*In a fun cartoon-ish fight,* CAPTAIN JUSTICE *and* MAELSTROM *work together to defeat* THE MOLE.)

THE MOLE: Okay, I was just kidding. You guys are really tough. Just don't hit me again, okay? Please?

(MAELSTROM *knocks him out.*)

CAPTAIN JUSTICE: Mal!

MAELSTROM: What?

CAPTAIN JUSTICE: He just asked you not to do that.

(*Focus shifts tightly on* MAELSTROM *again.*)

MAELSTROM: He was right. As the years went by, Jason did get good at being the icon. I however took a different route—A darker route. My town was in trouble—real trouble—the kind that didn't call for capes or fanfare. Like the rest of America, it needed saving bad—real bad. And I was willing to do anything to make sure that happened. I still am. That's why Jason and I have come to this point. This point right here.

(Fade to...)

MAELSTROM: This is where it all began, Helen.

HELEN: Where what began?

MAELSTROM: My birth.

HELEN: You were born here? Wow, that can't be hygienic.

MAELSTROM: My father died here, Helen. His blood right there where your feet stand. Execution style with a bullet in his brain.

HELEN: Jason never told me.

MAELSTROM: I brought you here to help you understand.

HELEN: Understand what?

MAELSTROM: Where I come from. Who and what I am. To hear my story.
   Do you know what the difference is between your husband and myself?

HELEN: You wear black and he wears blue?

MAELSTROM: Power. Real power. The kind that not only can save my city, but us all.

HELEN: He's a super and you're—

MAELSTROM: Just a man in a mask. I'm an imitator where he's the real deal. But where is he, Helen? Not here, not where it matters most. He's being Sam's lapdog.

HELEN: That's not fair, Mal. He's done good. You should see New York.

MAELSTROM: Have you ever wondered what the story of Jesus would be without his Judas? How could a God save humanity without his best friend's betrayal? Maybe the hero of that story isn't the son of Joseph, but the man who made that son a martyr.

HELEN: You sent that letter to me, didn't you?

MAELSTROM: Jason isn't a man, Helen. He's a God who hasn't accepted his immortality.

(HELEN *pulls out the gun and points it at* MAELSTROM.)

(*Fade to...*)

(CAPTAIN JUSTICE *enters.*)

CAPTAIN JUSTICE: Maelstrom, we need to talk.

MAELSTROM: Hey there, Boy Scout. I didn't know you made house calls.

CAPTAIN JUSTICE: There's five men in Saint Peter's Medical Center suffering near fatal injuries because of you.

MAELSTROM: Where's your jailbait?

CAPTAIN JUSTICE: Liberty is still in New York.

MAELSTROM: Could she not get out of school to travel?

CAPTAIN JUSTICE: Maelstrom, are listening to me? You're hurting people.

MAELSTROM: What's the big deal?

CAPTAIN JUSTICE: You're going too far.

MAELSTROM: Too far, Captain? How about not far enough? Do you know what those pieces of shit did? Do you?

CAPTAIN JUSTICE: No.

MAELSTROM: They're child predators, Cap. They rape children. Then again...you might be into that sort of thing.

CAPTAIN JUSTICE: I don't like what you're implying.

MAELSTROM: I'm not the one running around with a sixteen year old sidekick.

CAPTAIN JUSTICE: She's my partner.

MAELSTROM: She's your P R stunt.

CAPTAIN JUSTICE: You got to stop this, Mal. There's a line we can't cross and your dangling on it.

MAELSTROM: You make it sound like that's a bad thing.

CAPTAIN JUSTICE: It is.

MAELSTROM: Get out of my town, Captain. You can't just come here and start throwing judgements at me. This is my jurisdiction—I guard it the way I choose.

CAPTAIN JUSTICE: Mal—

MAELSTROM: GO.

CAPTAIN JUSTICE: You're terrorizing these people.

MAELSTROM: And I'm keeping them safe. If you spent more time patrolling these streets, instead of doing interviews and flying overseas, maybe you'd understand. Maybe you'd understand who really needs your help.

CAPTAIN JUSTICE: Anger is an easy route, Mal. Vengeance, spite, malice.

MAELSTROM: It's the only route.

CAPTAIN JUSTICE: You are coming with me.

MAELSTROM: You were there when my father passed, Jay. You know what this is for me. This is a war—a real war. One with the highest stakes. I've had casualties. I

pray you never have to know what this is like. This
pain. This guilt. It's been years and it only grows.
The men who killed my father now finally have a face
and it's all of them. Every single scumbag that points
a knife or a gun at an innocent. Every sicko who preys
on a child or woman. They all are my father's killer and
I'm going to stop them. They are all going to pay. If you
want to take me down, remember, you're letting them
win. You will be the reason they run rampant in my city.

(CAPTAIN JUSTICE *grabs* MAELSTROM *like he's going to
break him, but suddenly lets go.*)

CAPTAIN JUSTICE: What's happening to you, Mal?

MAELSTROM: I'm trying to save the world. Just like you.

(CAPTAIN JUSTICE *leaves.*)

(Fade to...)

HELEN: You're going down, Mal. The Honor Guard
isn't going to stand for this. You can't just throw out
fake threats whenever you like. I don't care what you
were trying to teach Jason, what you're doing is wrong.

MAELSTROM: He needed to know what it's like.

HELEN: By threatening me? Look, Mal, just cause he
doesn't do it with hate in his heart doesn't mean he
don't care. He is a hero whether you think he is or not.
Don't you move! *(She cocks the gun.)*

(MAELSTROM *walks right up to her.*)

MAELSTROM: You're not going to shoot me. You're too
much like your husband. You may bend rules, Helen,
but you're not ready to break them. Or am I wrong?

(HELEN *lowers her pistol.*)

HELEN: You're going to Steel City, Mal. They'll make
sure of it.

(MAELSTROM *exits.*)

(There's movement from afar.)

HELEN: *(Calling)* Hello? Are you still here? I'll shoot you in your fucking face, do you hear me? Do you?

(Suddenly, HURT and BURNOUT jump out of the shadows and grab her.)

BURNOUT: Hey, bitch. Remember us?

HELEN: No. Please.

BURNOUT: You shoulda got out of this town when you had the chance.

HELEN: Please. Let me go.

BURNOUT: This is the part where you scream.

(They drag her into the shadows.)

MAELSTROM: A bullet—a simple little bullet. It has the power to kill, but it also can create. It can re-create—transforming a man into a hero or a super back into a man...

(A scream)

(Gun shot!)

(Silence)

(Lights fade to black.)

INTERLUDE:
JUSTICE PART TWO

(Animated video sequence: Lights come up on a very comic bookish setting for CAPTAIN JUSTICE, LIBERTY LADY, and the HOODED MENACE.)

ANNOUNCER: Last we saw our heroes, they were face to face with Cap's sworn enemy—The Hooded Menace.

HOODED MENACE: Justice, this time I have the world in my clutches. One more step my way and I will use this remote detonating device to activate fifty nuclear missiles aimed at major cities across North America.

LIBERTY LADY: Golly, Cap, that would kill millions and millions of innocent lives.

CAPTAIN JUSTICE: Hooded Menace, what do you want?

HOODED MENACE: What does any super villain want? Not only do I want to take complete and utter control of this country, I also want something else.

LIBERTY LADY: Something else?

HOODED MENACE: I also want to finally annihilate its Superheroic champions forever.

CAPTAIN JUSTICE: You'll never be rid of us, we're like a bad smell that won't go away. And that smell, Menace, that smell is America!

LIBERTY LADY: You tell 'em Cap.

HOODED MENACE: That's what you think! Take this!

(HOODED MENACE *produces a second evil electronic device and activates it.* CAPTAIN JUSTICE *and* LIBERTY LADY *put their hands over their ears and writhe in pain.* HOODED MENACE *laughs with glee.*)

LIBERTY LADY: Cap, my ears. They hurt.

CAPTAIN JUSTICE: Mine too, Liberty. The pain is unbearable.

LIBERTY LADY: Menace must be using some kind of supersonic tone to scramble our super hearing.

HOODED MENACE: Hope you enjoy my little surprise, I designed it specially for you.

CAPTAIN JUSTICE: Can't focus. Sense of Justice weakening.

LIBERTY LADY: Super strength less super.

(HOODED MENACE *deactivates the evil device.*)

HOODED MENACE: Now that I've softened you up, I've invited a few more friends to finish the job. (*He speaks into his evil communicator.*)

LIBERTY LADY: Oh no, Cap, Menace's team of Norwegian Ninjas are surrounding us.

CAPTAIN JUSTICE: You have to be kidding me, Menace. Even with busted ear drums, we can still show these guys a true American welcome.

(CAPTAIN JUSTICE *and* LIBERTY LADY *fight the Ninjas and easily dispose of them in a very comic bookish fight.*)

HOODED MENACE: Impressive. However, though you may have defeated my Norwegian Ninjas, I still hold all North America hostage.

LIBERTY LADY: Oh no, Cap, he still has the detonator!

CAPTAIN JUSTICE: I have a plan. You distract him, while I knock that remote out of his hand with my SHIELD OF JUSTICE!

LIBERTY LADY: A weapon so Justi-rific it could even render you helpless.

CAPTAIN JUSTICE: Yes. Let us pray it never falls into the wrong hands.

HOODED MENACE: What are you two saying? No whispering!

CAPTAIN JUSTICE: Well, Liberty, I think the Hooded Menace has finally got us beat. I guess I'll just go and get the contracts from the President and hand over North America to Godlessness and Tyranny.

LIBERTY LADY: I'll miss fighting crime with you, Cap.

CAPTAIN JUSTICE: As will I. (*He pretends to leave.*)

HOODED MENACE: Finally! I win. I win. I win!

LIBERTY LADY: Well, Menace, I guess you won.

HOODED MENACE: Of course I would. Ha Ha Ha!

LIBERTY LADY: So, you want all of North America?
Even Canada and Mexico too?

HOODED MENACE: Actually, I didn't even think of those.

LIBERTY LADY: Don't worry. No one else does either.
That's quite a bit of land you're acquiring there.
Do you think you could spare a piece for a retiring
Super Hero's Faithful Sidekick?

HOODED MENACE: What are you implying?

LIBERTY LADY: You'll need someone to rule beside you.
I'm cute, you're the leader of an Underground
Organized Crime Ring. I think we would make
quite a lovely couple. Interested?

HOODED MENACE: Well, this is a bit awkward.
I thought it was obvious, but the thing is...have
you noticed how I like wearing spandex?

LIBERTY LADY: Now, Captain Justice!

CAPTAIN JUSTICE: Justice shield: fly!

(CAPTAIN JUSTICE *throws his shield at* HOODED MENACE
and knocks the remote out of his hands.)

HOODED MENACE: No!

CAPTAIN JUSTICE: Well, Menace, I guess you once again
underestimated the power of truth, justice and the
American Way.

HOODED MENACE: I was so close!

LIBERTY LADY: You were never close, Menace.

CAPTAIN JUSTICE: Menace, the only place you will be taking over will be behind the walls of a maximum-security prison. We're sending you to STEEL CITY!

HOODED MENACE: I'll get my revenge, Justice. Just wait and see. One day, I swear to you—I will bring you to your knees.

CAPTAIN JUSTICE: It looks like our job here is done, Lady. Let's go spread—

LIBERTY LADY: Liberty—

CAPTAIN JUSTICE: And Justice—

CAPTAIN JUSTICE & LIBERTY LADY: FOR ALL!!!

(End of video sequence)

SCENE II

(Projection: "Chapter Two: The Legend of Los Hermanos Manos")

(Projection: "Brooklyn, New York")

(Lights come up on MARCUS *dealing to* KING.*)*

MARCUS: This shit's the bomb, yo! You like to laugh? You like to laugh, son? Cause this shiznit right here will have you fuckin' rollin'.

KING: How much?

MARCUS: Two hunnerd.

KING: Two hunnerd for this shit?

MARCUS: This is premium stuff, dawg. This shit will have you trippin' old school. Like the Seventies, yo.

KING: I don't know.

MARCUS: I'm telling you, son—this gonna make you see some crazy ass hysterical shit. Like fuckin' killer

bunnies, hot singin' Laker bitches—this shit will make
you see God. Fuckin' God, yo. How you gonna deny
that?

KING: It's still expensive, dawg. I ain't gonna lie—
even for a trip like that.

MARCUS: Oh, I got you. You want to haggle. You one
of them haggling motherfuckers. Look, I'm giving you
a good price. I'm not fuckin' with you. You can't find
this shit just anywhere. So whatchoo you say?

(DAMON *and* LUKAS *jump out from the shadows.*
They are wearing Luchadore masks and silly capes.)

DAMON: Look! I spy drug dealers afoot!

LUKAS: Yo, man, I don't know about all this.

DAMON: Halt, criminals!

KING: Yo, whaddup with these circus clowns?

DAMON: Fool, we ain't no circus clowns. We're—
DAMON AND LUKAS LOS HERMANOS MANOS!

MARCUS: The hand brothers?

DAMON: And we're here to *hand* you our special brand
of justice!

(DAMON *and* LUKAS *storm towards* MARCUS *and* KING.)

(*They try to wrestle* MARCUS *and* KING *to the ground,*
but aren't very coordinated.)

(MARCUS *and* KING *reverse the attack and bind up* DAMON
and LUKAS.)

DAMON: Where did you learn that incredible move?

LUKAS: I told you this shit was dumb.

MARCUS: Alvarez? Damon Alvarez, is that you?

DAMON: No.

(MARCUS *and* KING *let go of the boys.*)

MARCUS: The fuck is all this about? Why y'all dressed up like it's Halloween?

KING: Maybe they into some kinky shit. *Pincha Maricones.*

LUKAS: Fuck you, son.

DAMON: We superheroes. Dedicated to keeping the streets clean of crime.

(MARCUS *and* KING *break out into hysterical laughter.*)

MARCUS: You what?

KING: You guys must be smoking some of that funny tobacco!

LUKAS: Yo, dawg, they laughing at us.

DAMON: We're crime fighters.

KING: Crime? You trying to fight crime?

DAMON: Yeah.

KING: Fuck you attacking us for?

LUKAS: Yo, man, you slingin' right here on the block. We saw it with our own eyes.

MARCUS: Nigga, I ain't slingin' shit.

LUKAS: What you got in your pocket then?

MARCUS: *Spamalot* tickets.

DAMON & LUKAS: *SPAMALOT?*

KING: My girl digs all that Broadway shit. Marcus here was hooking me up.

LUKAS: Yo. I told you Marcus don't sling no more.

MARCUS: Hey, Alvarez, your sister know you running around in your pajamas and shit?

DAMON: No.

MARCUS: Oh, shit, you didn't ask her?

DAMON: I don't need my sister's approval for everything. I'm the man of the house.

MARCUS: That girl is gonna tan that ass.

DAMON: She don't scare me.

MARCUS: Is that right?

DAMON: That's right.

(Fade to...)

*(*DAMON *and* LUKAS *with* CAMILLE. *She's pacing in front of them.)*

CAMILLE: What the fuck is wrong with you two? Seriously, what the fuck? Look at you! Have you two gone plain ass loco? Say something!

DAMON: We ain't crazy, Camille...

LUKAS: It's just a thing—

CAMILLE: SHUT UP! Why you want to embarrass me like this, huh? I got Marcus and King calling me— telling me you guys are running around attacking folks.

DAMON: We thought they was slinging.

CAMILLE: And what? You were gonna stop them? You cops now?

DAMON: Naw, Camille, it ain't like that.

CAMILLE: You actually walk around dressed like this? You're grown men.

DAMON: We luchadores, Camille. Heroes to the people and what not.

CAMILLE: Superheroes?

DAMON: Yeah.

LUKAS: *(Whispering)* Yo, Dawg, your sister's lookin' mighty pissed.

CAMILLE: What's your powers, Damon? You got powers? Can you fly, Damon? Can you fuckin' fly? How 'bout invisibility? Can you turn invisible?

DAMON: Naw, Camille, don't be retarded.

CAMILLE: How about indestructibility? You indestructible? Cause you better be hoping you're indestructible right about now!

(CAMILLE *throws a shoe at her brother.*)

DAMON: Yo, you crazy?

CAMILLE: You coulda gotten hurt. You coulda gotten killed! *Stupido, stupido, stupido!*

DAMON: I ain't stupid. You stupid.

LUKAS: Yo...

CAMILLE: What was that?

DAMON: I'm just sayin'—I can take care of myself. I don't need you.

CAMILLE: Yeah? Well, I better not see you and your stupid face in my house tonight!

DAMON: Your house? How you calling this your house? I lives here too!

LUKAS: Yo. Seriously, Dawg, I would not be debatin' your sister while she's in this state.

CAMILLE: Do you know what I do, Damon? Are you aware of what I fucking do everyday? I work in a bank, Damon. I have a respectable job working with respectable people. My visage is one demanding respect. I gots a good job—one that makes a good living to take care of us. To take care of you!

DAMON: Yo, why you gotta throw hate on me like that? Come out your mouth like I'm some bum?

CAMILLE: Cause you are, Damon. Cause you have—had one simple task and that task was go to school—learn something useful—get good grades...yet instead—you and your boy here rather run around looking like a pair of *pendejos* in Halloween costumes.

DAMON: Yo, step off—this shit here is classy. Fuckin' Luche Libre! *Viva la raza!*

CAMILLE: No, Damon, that shit is not classy. We're not even Mexican! This shit is ignorant.

DAMON: How you gonna say that?

CAMILLE: This is the shit that my respectable co-workers think of me—of us.
Tacos—lowriders—hoop earrings and big butts—this is the shit that keeps us down, Damon, not lift us up. This is a dead, unimportant, harmful stereotypical bullshit that shackles down our people. This isn't making anyone stronger. This here is what makes us weak.

(Fade to DAMON *and* LUKAS *sitting on some steps.)*

LUKAS: Yo, D, maybe your sister's right. You gotta admit, this shit is kinda ridiculous.

DAMON: It's not ridiculous.

LUKAS: I'm just saying—

DAMON: Did you see the paper this morning, Luke?

LUKAS: Naw.

DAMON: Midtown got attacked by a robot.

LUKAS: Say what?

DAMON: A huge motherfuckin' robot. I'm talking big Godzilla motherfucka—fuckin' Rodan and shit.

Stormin' thru, crushin' cars—fuckin' shit up left and right. And then you know what happened?

LUKAS: What?

DAMON: Fuckin' Captain Justice and Liberty Lady show up.

LUKAS: Yo, that bitch is fine.

DAMON: No doubt. Fuckin' came in, ran through that thing like it was built out of lego blocks.

LUKAS: Fuck.

DAMON: And do you know how many people got hurt?

LUKAS: Coupla dozen prolly?

DAMON: Zero. A big fuckin' goose egg. Not one motherfucka got a scratch. While Captain Justice was doing his thing, Liberty Lady was running around saving tourists, babies, fuckin' Broadway actors.
    Folks were standing in the street cheering. Motherfuckin' Robot come down my street, you know my ass be bookin' it. But no—these motherfucka's takin' photos with their cellphones, fuckin' callin' up their homeboy to watch it live on C N N and shit. They gots no fear cause they know Captain J is here.

LUKAS: Dumbass white folks.

DAMON: Look anywhere—every paper, every day— front page has been the same thing for over a decade— some super is saving somebody somewhere in this city—kids, grandmas, fuckin' kitties from trees. Yo, this town is safer than a fuckin' Disney park ride.

LUKAS: Word.

DAMON: Yet you flip to the back of any of these papers, what you got?

LUKAS: Classifieds?

DAMON: Police Log. Crime. Not front page shit—
real shit. Murders, assault, rape. All where? Ain't
in Manhattan—ain't in Gramercy Park or the West
Village. Fuckin' here—Bushwick. Fuckin' here—
the Bronx, Crown Heights. Fuckin' here—where
the ratio of white folks is damn near zero.
   That's why we wear these masks—cause none
of those motherfuckers are coming here. If someone
is gonna keep these streets safe, it's gonna be us.
Los Hermanos Manos.

LUKAS: Yeah.

DAMON: So fuck my sister.

LUKAS: Yeah!

DAMON: Fuck her respectable job up in the city.

LUKAS: That too!

DAMON: Fuck all that. We keepin' this shit real.

LUKAS: Yo, dawg, not to shit on your pride parade,
but we ain't never helped nobody so far.

DAMON: Shhhh. We will. We just—well, we just gotta
figure out what our powers are first.

LUKAS: Can we get guns in the meantime?

DAMON: Yeah, maybe.

(Fade to...)

*(CAMILLE coming home from work. ANDERSON is waiting
on her steps.)*

ANDERSON: Yo, Camille. Baby.

CAMILLE: What the fuck you doing here?

ANDERSON: What's with the hostility? Just sayin' hi.

CAMILLE: Get outta my way.

ANDERSON: Look, I know we've been having some problems, but we can work it out. I love you, baby.

CAMILLE: You're drunk.

ANDERSON: I'm off-duty. A man off-duty is allowed a drink every now and again.

CAMILLE: Except every now and again, you get nasty.

ANDERSON: *(Through laughter)* I didn't realize you was such a prude.

CAMILLE: Don't you fuckin' laugh at me. I'm not making a joke.

ANDERSON: I just find it funny.

CAMILLE: Oh, do you? You find this humourous? This is like a humorous situation to you? Talking to me is like what—an episode of *The Simpsons* or something? I'm like a cartoon?

ANDERSON: No.

CAMILLE: Then stop laughing at me.

ANDERSON: Damn, baby, I miss that.

CAMILLE: You miss what?

ANDERSON: That Latin heat of yours. That fire. Come here.

CAMILLE: Get off of me, Bobby. I told you that this is over. You have lost all touching privileges. My body is off limits to you and your hands.

ANDERSON: Well, then there's other parts that can touch.

CAMILLE: Is that what you think?

ANDERSON: That's what I had in mind.

CAMILLE: Pull it out. See what happens.

(Beat)

ANDERSON: Damn, Camille, you can't really be serious about breaking up.

CAMILLE: Bobby, a relationship is two people who want to be together. Stress on the word "want". As in you want to be with me and I want to be with you.

ANDERSON: That's what I'm talking about.

CAMILLE: However—I don't want to be with you, Bobby. You're all...different now.

ANDERSON: Camille, you were the one who said you wanted to know about my fantasies.

CAMILLE: Yeah.

ANDERSON: So this is kind of your fault. You opened Pandora's box.

CAMILLE: I don't know who the hell Pandora is, but I damn well did not touch her box!

ANDERSON: It's an expression.

CAMILLE: I don't give a shit what it is...you're wrong. Get out of here.

ANDERSON: I'm not wrong, Camille. We were talking about sex—the theme to our conversation was sexual in nature—all questions and responses were about sex...what did you think I was going to say? My greatest fantasy is to only fuck you for the rest of my life?

(CAMILLE *gives* ANDERSON *a glare.*)

ANDERSON: Okay, perhaps that was the wrong thing to say.

CAMILLE: Get outta my way, Bobby. Get the fuck out of here or I'm gonna call a cop.

ANDERSON: I am a cop.

CAMILLE: Then I'll call my cousins. They fucking hate cops.

ANDERSON: Camille, I'm sorry, okay? I'm sorry this wigs you out. But alot of guys have this fantasy. Alot. It's actually quite mundane.

CAMILLE: No, Bobby. Mundane is wanting to sleep with two girls or be tied up or doing it in some strange geographical location. That's a mundane fantasy.

ANDERSON: I just said I wanted to sleep with a superhero, I didn't expect you to get so worked up.

CAMILLE: Well, I'm not a superhero, Bobby. There is no way I'm ever going to be a superhero. Not even if you threw me in a vat of toxic waste and an army of radioactive bugs came and bit the shit out of me. If you want to be with a superhero so bad, go find one. I don't care.

(Fade to...)

*(*DAMON *and* LUKAS *on the subway.)*

DAMON: Pardon this interruption, my name is Damon and this my boy—Luke—and we here selling candy for some basketball uniforms for our basketball team. We gots peanut M & Ms and Starbursts for a dollar. If you're not feeling up to candy this evening, we also take donations. Any help will be greatly appreciated. Thank you and God Bless.

LUKAS: *(Approaching a female audience member)*
Hey, whazzup, pretty girl? You want some candy? Something sticky. Sweet. Melts in your mouth like a lemon drop. You like that, don't you? You feelin' me.

DAMON: Luke.

LUKAS: In a minute, I'm busy.

DAMON: Lukas.

LUKAS: *(To girl)* Ignore him. I don't know that dude. He's weird, ain't he? So, you wanna give me your digits. It's alright, I'll wait.

DAMON: LUKE!

LUKAS: *(To girl)* Excuse me. *(To* DAMON*)* What, man? What? My game is on and you cock-blocking me.

DAMON: The fuck are you doing?

LUKAS: What's it look like, son? I'm selling candy.

DAMON: Will you act serious?

LUKAS: I am acting serious.

DAMON: Real serious.

LUKAS: Oh. You want "real serious"?

DAMON: Yes.

LUKAS: Alright, then. *(To a different audience member)* Yo, dude, give me a motherfuckin' dollar before I kick that ass!

*(*DAMON *runs up and pulls* LUKAS *away.)*

DAMON: Luke, what the fuck?

LUKAS: You said act real serious. What the fuck do you think that was? Check it—I was so serious that dude almost pissed himself.

DAMON: How much you sold?

LUKAS: What?

DAMON: I said, how much have you sold?

LUKAS: Lots. Tons. I'm about to put Willy Wonka out of business.

DAMON: Where's the money?

LUKAS: In my pocket.

DAMON: Let me see it.

LUKAS: Naw.

DAMON: Let. Me. See. It.

LUKAS: Aw, fuck you, man. This shit is gay.

DAMON: It's making us money.

LUKAS: Man, nobody's gonna believe we part of no basketball team.

DAMON: You got a better plan?

LUKAS: Maybe.

DAMON: Maybe.

LUKAS: This sucks, D. This is like high school bullshit. Fuckers who still got zits and can't control their boners do this shit. Seriously, how much you think you can make selling fucking Peanut M & Ms?

DAMON: I don't know.

LUKAS: Yo, you know how much candy we gotta sell to be able to afford some guns? I'm talking good guns—not some street shit that'll just blow up all in your face? That shit's expensive.

DAMON: Yo, maybe Camille's right. This superhero stuff is stupid.

(Fade to...)

*(*ANDERSON *and* CAMILLE *still outside)*

ANDERSON: Look, I don't want you to be a superhero, Camille. I was just telling you what I think about on occasion. Note the term "On occasion". Not frequently. It's like wanting to bone a celebrity, there's no chance of that ever happening. It's a silly unimportant fantasy.

CAMILLE: We're different people, Bobby.

ANDERSON: Why? Why are we so different? What do you want? What is your big sexual desire, huh? Do you want to sleep with a ton of guys? A woman? What?

CAMILLE: It's not about fantasies, Bobby. It's about how we see the world.

ANDERSON: I swear to you, Camille, wanting to bone Liberty Lady has zero reflection on my outlook on the world.

CAMILLE: No, Bobby, it hugely speaks to how you see it.

ANDERSON: It's my dick, Camille. I don't see the world through my dick. My dick doesn't have a brain, it has no opinion—no power. I do something, it comes along. It's attached, but it don't lead. It's mainly just a really nice accessory for fucking and peeing.

CAMILLE: Bobby, when you think of Captain Justice, what pops in your head?

ANDERSON: I told you I don't want to fuck Captain Justice. I want to fuck Liberty Lady. Stress on the female superheroes here, please.

CAMILLE: That's not what I mean. When you think of Captain Justice, what do you think?

ANDERSON: I don't know. America. Red, White, and Blue. He's a good guy.

CAMILLE: And Maelstrom?

ANDERSON: Another good guy. What's your point?

CAMILLE: Bobby, that's where we differ.

ANDERSON: You don't think they're good?

CAMILLE: We're different people.

ANDERSON: Wait, you actually think supers are bad? That's crazy. They're superheroes, Camille. Note the word HERO in that expression. Meaning, they are good. If not, they'd be call Superpeople or "superfolks", something generic to signify their neutrality on the existential scale between right and wrong.

CAMILLE: Go home.

ANDERSON: No.

CAMILLE: Go.

ANDERSON: Camille, this is a pretty fucking ridiculous reason to break up a relationship.

CAMILLE: Is it?

ANDERSON: Yes.

CAMILLE: Bobby, when's the last time you had to spend any real time in a hospital?

ANDERSON: I don't know.

CAMILLE: When was the last time you had to sit in a waiting room because one of you cops got all shot up?

ANDERSON: It's been a long time.

CAMILLE: When's the last time you knew anyone who died because of a super?

ANDERSON: Camille, did someone you know get hurt by one of them?

CAMILLE: Someone? Try everyone in this fucking hood, Bobby. It's nice that you think that supers are heroes. That's nice. Real nice. But that shit ain't universal. They're no heroes to us. They only worry about saving folks in the city or overseas—commercial areas where they can get photo ops and publicity. They don't give a shit about us on the fringe.

ANDERSON: So you're pissed that they don't patrol Bushwick, is that what this is all about?

CAMILLE: No, I'm pissed because every single thug, criminal, and lowlife that once lived over there has

come here because they know they can run freely
without interference. Because everyone has gotten
so dependent on heroes, no one is keeping an eye out
anymore. Cops are getting drunk in the middle of their
shifts to deal with their girlfriends and when shit does
hit the fan—it's not you who has to deal with it. It's us.
Boys here are getting killed left and right tryin' to take
up the slack that you officers have let go and that the
heroes ignore. So no, Bobby, it's not just a fantasy,
it's a bullshit reality that exists for you, but not for
me and that's what make us different. That's why
we can't be together no more.

ANDERSON: No, Camille, please. Let me try to make
it up to you. Let me try to make it work. There has to
be something.

CAMILLE: Go do your job.

ANDERSON: Okay, okay. I'm gonna clean up this hood,
Camille. I will. You'll see.

(Focus shifts to MARCUS *and* KING.*)*

MARCUS: King, these ain't going to last forever.
They time sensitive. So we got a deal or what?

KING: Fine. But these seats better be close. I'm talking
real close—like I can see fuckin' nose hairs and shit.
Fuckin' pores and what not? I want Hank Azaria to be
spittin' on my girl when he talks. She better be gettin'
spat on, you know what I'm saying?

MARCUS: She will, she will. These are nice, yo. They in
the mezzanine.

KING: What's a mezzanine?

MARCUS: It's French for like "really fuckin' close".
Actually mezzanine translates into "Area in which
niggas get spat on". That's how close they is.

KING: Cool. That's what I'm talking about.

MARCUS: So we got a deal?

KING: Yeah, we got a deal.

MARCUS: Sweet tits.

(KING *palms the money over to* MARCUS.)

(*Suddenly,* ANDERSON *[by the way,* ANDERSON *should not be in uniform or this scene won't make any sense] steps up from behind them with a gun pointed.*)

ANDERSON: Hey, guys, what are you up to?

MARCUS: Yo, man, what the fuck?

ANDERSON: What you got there, huh? Something illegal?

MARCUS: Dude, you can have whatever you want.

ANDERSON: You think I want anything from you, asshole? I don't want shit from you. I just want you to get the fuck out of this neighborhood.

MARCUS: What?

ANDERSON: You heard me.

KING: Look, man, I got like two hundred cash on me, it's all yours. Take it.

ANDERSON: You trying to bribe me, scumbag?

KING: That's exactly what I'm trying to do. You like my kicks? You can have them too. How 'bout my jacket?

ANDERSON: I don't take bribes.

KING: What you mean you don't take bribes? Everybody takes bribes.

ANDERSON: I don't.

(ANDERSON *slugs* KING *in the stomach.* KING *falls to the ground.*)

(DAMON *and* LUKAS *enter.*)

(LUKAS *sees that* MARCUS *and* KING *are in trouble.*)

LUKAS: Yo, D, check it.

DAMON: What the fuck?

LUKAS: You wanted to build some rep, right? That big dude is mugging our boys over there.

DAMON: Holy fuck, we should go tell somebody.

LUKAS: Ain't nobody to tell, D. We Los Hermanos Manos, let's go hand that motherfucker an asskicking.

DAMON: What?

LUKAS: This is what you've been talking about.

DAMON: I don't know.

LUKAS: Come on, D, this is our chance. So you in the mood to fuck up some evil?

DAMON: Uh...

LUKAS: I said—are you in the mood to fuck up some evil?

DAMON: Yeah. Hell's yeah.

LUKAS: Well, let's go then...

(DAMON *and* LUKAS *sneak off.*)

MARCUS: Yo, man, I'm telling ya—I just got tickets on me. I don't got any drugs.

ANDERSON: I don't believe you.

MARCUS: Dude, I don't sling.

ANDERSON: WHERE ARE THEY?

MARCUS: No where. I have no drugs.

ANDERSON: Don't fucking lie to me, you fucking reptile.

MARCUS: I'm not.

(ANDERSON *nails* MARCUS. MARCUS *falls to the ground.*)

(DAMON *and* LUKAS *jump in.*)

LUKAS: Yo, punk, get your hands off our boy.

(ANDERSON *turns to see* LUKAS *and* DAMON, *but before* ANDERSON *can react,* LUKAS *bumrushes him and starts fighting.*)

(ANDERSON's *gun falls to the ground.* DAMON *recovers it.*)

(ANDERSON *reverses the momentum and begins beating on* LUKAS.)

(DAMON *cocks the gun and points it at* ANDERSON.)

DAMON: FREEZE! Turn around. DON'T MOVE! (*To* LUKAS) Are you okay? (*To* ANDERSON) Help him up...yes, give him your hand—you hurt him pretty bad. Now say you're sorry. Say it.

ANDERSON: I'm sorry.

LUKAS: It's okay. You're a worthy adversary.

(LUKAS *hugs* ANDERSON.)

DAMON: (*To* LUKAS) Why you hugging him, dawg? He just beat your ass. Come here. Let me look at that. He hit you in the eye. That's going to swell. Do you think you have a concussion? You might be brain damaged. Do you feel brain damaged? How many fingers am I holding up?

(*BANG! The gun accidentally goes off and hits* ANDERSON *square in the chest.*)

(DAMON *and* LUKAS *duck thinking someone is firing at them. They look at each other and then at* ANDERSON.)

(ANDERSON *falls dead.*)

DAMON & LUKAS: OOOOOOOOOOH...SHIT.

(*Sirens blare in the distance.*)

(*Lights fade...*)

INTERLUDE:
JUSTICE PART THREE

(Animated video sequence: We see comic book images depicting the death of HURT *and* BURNOUT.*)*

(Lights come up on CAPTAIN JUSTICE *and the City's* DISTRICT ATTORNEY *(D A).)*

D A: So tell us, Captain Justice, in your own words—what exactly happened on the night of October 17th, 2005?

(Lights come up on two hoodlums, HURT *and* BURNOUT, *in an alley way.* HURT *is drenched in blood.)*

HURT: Oh man! Oh man! We're screwed!

BURNOUT: Pipe down, will ya? We're not screwed.

HURT: Why the fuck did we have do that, man?

BURNOUT: We're gonna be fine, Hurt. We're gonna be fine. This ain't a thing.

HURT: This ain't a thing? Look at me. I look like a fuckin' human tampon, what do you mean it ain't a thing? I got that bitch's blood all over me.

D A: What were you doing in Chicago, Captain Justice? Were you trying to stop a crime? Were you just patrolling? Or were you there for revenge?

HURT: Why did we have to whack her, man? So what? She just kicked our ass, who cares? Now we got some pissed off super after us.

BURNOUT: Calm down.

HURT: We gotta go find us a bus, man.

BURNOUT: A bus?

HURT: Or a cab. Subway. Somethin. We just gotta get the hell outta here. And fast.

D A: At what point did you encounter Thomas Hurt and Bernie Dalton? What did you say to them?

HURT: Yo, man, he ain't gonna kill us, right? He ain't like Maelstrom. He ain't crazy, right?

D A: Did they have any powers, Captain Justice? Any special skills or attributes? Or were they just regular citizens? People like myself—like the jury—who are completely defenseless against an individual much like yourself.

(CAPTAIN JUSTICE *walks into the scene with* HURT *and* BURNOUT.)

HURT: Burnout...

D A: What did they do, Captain Justice? Why use such force? Where you ever planning on arresting them, Captain?

(The two men spot CAPTAIN JUSTICE.*)*

HURT: Fuck, man. Oh fuck! It's Captain Justice.

CAPTAIN JUSTICE/JASON: Blood.

HURT: Oh, fuck me. Fuck me. I told you, man. I fuckin' told you!

D A: What was your approach? Did you obey procedure? Did you read them their rights?

BURNOUT: Yo, man, we didn't do anything. This is just a misunderstanding.

D A: Did you give them an option to surrender?

CAPTAIN JUSTICE/JASON: You lie. Your kind always lie.

BURNOUT: We ain't fuckin' lying!

CAPTAIN JUSTICE/JASON: I smell her sweat on you. I see her blood.

BURNOUT: No, it's not what you think—

D A: Remember, Captain, you are under oath.

(CAPTAIN JUSTICE *suddenly attacks both men. He throws them behind a dumpster. We only see their shadows and blood spraying onto the alleyway's walls.*)

(*A spotlight rises on a bloody* CAPTAIN JUSTICE. *He is drenched.*)

(CAPTAIN JUSTICE *raises his face so we can see him.*)

CAPTAIN JUSTICE/JASON: Justice was served.

(*End of video sequence*)

SCENE III

(*Projection: "Chapter Three: The Tragic Tale of Bryant the Indestructible"*)

(*Projection: "Mobile, Alabama."*)

(*Spotlight on* BRYANT, *a large man poorly dressed like a woman—bad wig, bad lipstick, a horrid dress. He sits in a run-down motel room.*)

(JOE DICKENS *enters from a bathroom, straightening his tie. He's a smoothly dressed businessman.*)

JOE DICKENS: I gotta tell ya, kid, that was something else. That was really—wow. That was like some Junior High School fantasy shit. The guys—they talk about it—they brag. You know—locker room shit. But, fuck, hitting you—just fucking kicking your ass was—I like that you scream—that's a nice touch—classy—I know it's an act an' all—but, fuck, I really appreciate it. It's good for the ego, you know. Ain't no fun beating the shit out of a motherfucker and have them just stand there.

   I can't believe you exist, man—I can't believe God in all his greatness decided to make something like you. Have you always been like this or did you come from outer space or somethin'?

(BRYANT *does not answer.*)

JOE DICKENS: Alright then. I will see you later, man. I will fucking see you later. Thanks for a great night. A great fuckin' night.

BRYANT: This is not who I always was.

MOTHER: *(O S)* Baby.

BRYANT: I once was much smaller.

(*Lights fade only on* BRYANT.)

(*It's years ago.*)

(MOTHER *enters.*)

MOTHER: Baby, why are you dressed like that?

BRYANT: I look pretty, Mommy. Don't I? Don't I look pretty?

MOTHER: Bryant, take that off.

BRYANT: But, Mommy, I'm dressed like you.

MOTHER: You know what'll happen if your daddy sees this...

BRYANT: He won't, Mommy. He won't. I'm pretty though, ain't I? Ain't I pretty?

(MOTHER *examines her boy quietly.*)

MOTHER: Yes, you are, darlin'. You're a very very pretty girl.

BRYANT: Can I try make-up? I wanna wear make-up, Mommy.

MOTHER: You want to wear what?

BRYANT: I want to wear purple make-up around my eyes like you. *(He points at* MOTHER'*s eyes.)* Makes you look like a big raccoon!

MOTHER: Honey, you don't want that.

BRYANT: But I do. I wanna be just like you.

MOTHER: No, Bryant.

BRYANT: But—

MOTHER: Bryant, NO.

BRYANT: I'm sorry, Mommy.

MOTHER: Bryant, do you know what hurt is?

BRYANT: No, Mommy.

MOTHER: It's like when your Daddy yells at you. You know that feeling, right? Deep inside. What's it feel inside?

BRYANT: Not good.

MOTHER: Well, imagine that, but on top of your skin. That's hurt. That's where the purple comes from.

BRYANT: I don't like hurt.

MOTHER: Well, you never have to worry about that. God made you special, honey.

BRYANT: Like you?

MOTHER: Not just like me. You and me are special in different ways.

BRYANT: But I want to be like you, Mommy. I wanna be strong.

MOTHER: You are, baby. In here, you are.

BRYANT: Why do you let Daddy make you hurt?

MOTHER: Cause, Bryant, Mommy doesn't want to do something bad.

(MOTHER *gently places her hand on* BRYANT's *chest and gives him a kiss on the forehead.*)

(*Lights quickly shift back to* JOE DICKENS *kicking the shit out of* BRYANT.)

(*Several men stand around impatiently waiting.*)

(MOTHER *is gone.*)

JOE DICKENS: Fuck you, bitch! You wanna spend my dough? You wanna spend my hard earned cash on fuckin' clothes? Fuckin' jewelry? You wanna know why I ain't buying you shit?

REYNOLDS: Yo, man, let me get a turn.

JOE DICKENS: Just one more.

(JOE DICKENS *kicks* BRYANT *in the gut.*)

JOE DICKENS: And that is for having your mother spend Christmas at our house!

(JOE DICKENS *picks up and holds* BRYANT *for* REYNOLDS *to hit.*)

JOE DICKENS: Get you some of this, Reynolds.

REYNOLDS: I got those copies you asked for. (*He kicks* BRYANT *in the crotch.*) Hey, why don't you fuckin' walk your own goddamn fat ass down to the copy center, huh? You big sloppy sack of shit?

(REYNOLDS *tags* CHRISTIAN *in.*)

CHRISTIAN: Yeah, Bobby, I'm fuckin' your wife. You got a problem with that? I like fucking—NO—I love fucking her. But you...you I just want to fuck up!

(CHRISTIAN *pounds on* BRYANT.)

(CHRISTIAN *tags back in* REYNOLDS.)

JOE DICKENS: Fuck you, Mom!

REYNOLDS: Fuck you, Dad!

CHRISTIAN: Fuck you, Baby Jesus!

(Each man punctuates his point with a brutal hit.)

*(*BRYANT *lies on the floor crying.)*

(The men pull money from their wallets and drop it on BRYANT.*)*

(As they leave, BRYANT *immediately stops crying and picks up his day's earnings.)*

(Fade to…)

MOTHER: Bryant, put away your toys and clean up before—

DADDY: What is this? What's is that he's wearing?

MOTHER: We were just playing dress-up.

DADDY: Does he know that Mommy's things are for girls?

MOTHER: I don't see the harm—he's just playin'.

DADDY: Bryant, take that shit off.

BRYANT: But I like it.

DADDY: Take it off now, boy.

BRYANT: Yes, sir.

MOTHER: Don't get hostile. He don't know better.

DADDY: I'm trying to take care of both of you. Do you understand that?

MOTHER: Yes, dear.

DADDY: You need to teach him. He needs to understand about right and wrong. He needs to know the proper way to act in civilized society. And he needs to know that the shit he gots on right now has no place in it.

MOTHER: *(To* BRYANT*)* Come here, baby. Let me help you take that off.

DADDY: You're going to be that boy's undoin'.

BRYANT: Daddy's mad. Is he gonna make you purple again?

DADDY: What you talking about, Bryant? What does Daddy make Mommy?

BRYANT: Purple. Purple make-up on her eyes. Makes her look like a raccoon. A cute little raccoon.

DADDY: Did you tell him this?

MOTHER: I messed up, okay?

DADDY: Come here, woman.

MOTHER: I'm sorry.

DADDY: Don't make me ask you again.

(MOTHER *slowly walks to* DADDY.)

DADDY: It's been a long time since you've needed one of these. You need a little remindin'.

MOTHER: No, please.

(*He rears back his hand to hit* MOTHER.)

(*Lights shift on* BRYANT *alone in a hotel room. He has a shopping bag. He turns it over and dumps out a series of knives.*)

(*He picks them up one by one and jabs them into himself. They break on contact.*)

BRYANT: Bad boy. Bryant is a bad boy. Bad bad boy. (*He stares at all the broken metal.*)

(MELINDA *enters. She's a very hot, very seductive call-girl.*)

MELINDA: Hey, sugah, did you call for some room service? Cause I'm Melinda and I'm here to serve.

BRYANT: They all broke. They always break.

MELINDA: Uh...I don't know what you got planned, but I don't do that—whatever that is.

BRYANT: I'm suppose to wait here for some people.

MELINDA: People?

BRYANT: People.

MELINDA: Look, guy, I don't do groups. Just one on one stuff. No offense, I'm just still kinda...new at this.

BRYANT: New at what?

MELINDA: Why are you dressed like that?

BRYANT: Like what?

MELINDA: Like that—like you're...Tammy Faye Bakker?

BRYANT: I'm a woman.

MELINDA: You are obviously not a woman.

BRYANT: I look like a woman.

MELINDA: Not to pee in your Kool-Aid, sweetheart, but you don't look anything like a woman.

BRYANT: That's what they like. The men.

MELINDA: The men?

BRYANT: The men that hit me. They like it when I dress like this.

MELINDA: Are you alright?

BRYANT: What do you mean?

MELINDA: Are you hurt? Is that what this all about? Did you bring this to protect you from the men? The men that hit you?

BRYANT: I can't get hurt.

MELINDA: Look, I know what it's like. To get hit. Let me help you.

BRYANT: I don't need help.

MELINDA: Sometimes we all need—

BRYANT: Look. See? *(He grabs another knife and jabs himself with it. It breaks.)*

MELINDA: Holy. Shit.

BRYANT: I can't get hurt.

MELINDA: Holy fucking shit—you're...you're—

BRYANT: God made me special.

MELINDA: You're a super!

BRYANT: What's a super?

MELINDA: Like Captain Justice.

BRYANT: Who?

MELINDA: People in the news. Up north.

BRYANT: You're pretty. You look like a princess.

MELINDA: I look like a what?

BRYANT: Your dress. It makes you look all bright— like a billboard.

MELINDA: I think it's a bit cheesy, but—well, my boss thinks guys'll like it. Does it work?

BRYANT: It's nice.

MELINDA: Thanks.

BRYANT: Why are you here? Did you come to hit me?

MELINDA: No! No. I was told to be here. I think you're in my room.

BRYANT: Your room?

MELINDA: Not my room, but some Midwestern banker's—

BRYANT: Do you want me to go?

MELINDA: Nah, it's alright. Whoever called must have bailed. Guess this little girl is dieting for yet another night.

BRYANT: But you're skinny.

MELINDA: Irony doesn't work on you, does it?

BRYANT: What?

MELINDA: Never mind.
So you let people hit you?

BRYANT: For money.

MELINDA: Wow, and I thought what I did was bad.

BRYANT: I like you.

MELINDA: I like you too.

BRYANT: My name is Bryant.

MELINDA: I'm Melinda.

BRYANT: What do you do, Melinda?

MELINDA: I'm in...sales.

BRYANT: You sell stuff? Like what?

MELINDA: Sort of the same thing as you do.

BRYANT: We don't have good jobs, do we?

MELINDA: No, Bryant, we don't. We certainly don't.

(Fade to...)

*(*JOE DICKENS, REYNOLDS, *and* CHRISTIAN *hanging out on the corner.)*

REYNOLDS: The fuck, man. I can't believe "Fight Club" bailed on us tonight.

CHRISTIAN: I had this whole scenario set up involving my ninth grade algebra teacher. Fuckin' fat bitch. Now, it's ruined.

REYNOLDS: Tell me about it.

CHRISTIAN: I was gonna smack the shit out of her with this here ruler. DAMN! Now I ain't got nothin' to do with it.

REYNOLDS: Maybe next time.

CHRISTIAN: I guess I could go to the gym and work it off. What about you guys?

REYNOLDS: The gym might be good. Hit the old bags.

JOE DICKENS: NO! No. We came to kick some ass, we should do it.

REYNOLDS: Dude, we can't. Your boy bailed.

JOE DICKENS: Just cause we can't hit that retard doesn't mean we can't party.

REYNOLDS: Dude, what are you saying?

JOE DICKENS: Let's go pick a fight.

REYNOLDS: Are you fucking crazy?

JOE DICKENS: Oh, come on. It'll just be a bar brawl. People get into bar brawls all the time.

CHRISTIAN: I don't.

REYNOLDS: Me neither.

JOE DICKENS: Come on, you pussies. Let's just start some shit. Raise some hell. It'll be like college again. Kappa Kappa Kick some ass.

CHRISTIAN: Joe, listen to yourself

REYNOLDS: Look, dude, you should just go home. Hang out with your wife or something, man. You're talking all crazy.

CHRISTIAN: We'll try to find your guy next week.

JOE DICKENS: Yeah, next week.

REYNOLDS: Dude, it's not that bad. Go home.

(REYNOLDS *and* CHRISTIAN *leave.*)

(*Lights come up on* MELINDA *on a corner.*)

(JOE DICKENS *approaches.*)

MELINDA: Hey, sugah, wanna party?

JOE DICKENS: What?

MELINDA: You look lonely, stranger. What's your name?

JOE DICKENS: Joe.

MELINDA: I'm Melinda. No one should be lonely on a night like tonight. Wanna go unwind?

JOE DICKENS: Yeah. Yeah, I'd love to unwind.

MELINDA: I don't do anything kinky. Just straight, okay? That fine?

JOE DICKENS: Definitely. I definitely could go for something straight.

MELINDA: Okay. Come on.

JOE DICKENS: No.
   I have a place. It's nice.

(*Fade to...*)

(DADDY *on the ground. He lies completely motionless.*)

BRYANT: Daddy?

MOTHER: Don't touch him, Bryant. Daddy needs to sleep.

BRYANT: Daddy? Get up.

MOTHER: Bryant, I said leave him be.

BRYANT: What did you do, Mommy?

MOTHER: Mommy did a bad thing. Mommy hit Daddy.

BRYANT: You hit him and this happened?

MOTHER: Your Mommy hits pretty hard when she's mad.
  I guess we're more alike than you thought.

BRYANT: Is he gonna be alright?

MOTHER: You should go to your room. I'll bring the T.V. in there. You can watch cartoons.

BRYANT: Mommy, is he gonna be okay?

MOTHER: I don't know, Bryant. I don't think so.

(BRYANT *goes to his* MOTHER. *She hugs him.*)

(*Lights up on* MELINDA *and* JOE DICKENS. *They barge into the hotel room.* JOE DICKENS *throws her against a wall. She bounces off it like a rubber ball.*)

JOE DICKENS: I should have never fucking married you, you fucking bitch!

MELINDA: I'm not your wife. Why are you doing this?

JOE DICKENS: You tricked me. You suffocated me. If it weren't for you, I'd be someone else—something else—greater than this.

MELINDA: You're crazy.

JOE DICKENS: No, baby, I'm just being me.

MOTHER: I think I might have to go away for awhile, baby. Do you understand?

(BRYANT *shakes his head.*)

MOTHER: It's gonna be alright. You gotta promise me something, okay? Don't do what Mommy just did. If the world wants to hit you, Bryant, you let 'em.

MELINDA: Please leave me alone!

MOTHER: You take every hit, every smack, and you find a way to make something good out of it. That's why God made you this way.

JOE DICKENS: We gonna have some fun.

MOTHER: You're special, you can take it. Don't hurt anyone, okay?

BRYANT: I love you, Mommy.

JOE DICKENS: I hate you.

MOTHER: I love you too, Bryant. You are my very pretty little girl.

(MOTHER *walks away.* JOE DICKENS *pulls his belt off.*)

MELINDA: What are you going to do with that?

JOE DICKENS: Daddy's going to give you a little spanking.

MELINDA: No. Please.

JOE DICKENS: Get up.

MELINDA: No.

JOE DICKENS: I said get up, bitch.

(BRYANT *enters the scene.*)

BRYANT: Leave her alone.

(JOE DICKENS *turns to see* BRYANT.)

BRYANT: I said leave her alone.

JOE DICKENS: There you are! There you fucking are! Where the fuck were you, huh? We were looking to party with you all night!

MELINDA: Bryant...

JOE DICKENS: What? You think this fucking retard is going to help you? He loves getting smacked around. Don't you? Don't you, you big fucking stupid shit.

(JOE DICKENS *steps towards* MELINDA. BRYANT *grabs* JOE DICKENS.)

BRYANT: God made me special.

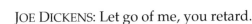

JOE DICKENS: Let go of me, you retard.

BRYANT: You ain't gonna hurt her.

JOE DICKENS: I said let me go.

BRYANT: No more hurt. No more hurting folks,
you hear me.

JOE DICKENS: Let go, goddammit!

(*As* JOE DICKENS *tries to struggle out of* BRYANT's *grasp,*
MELINDA *picks a knife out of* BRYANT's *bag. She looks up
and stabs* JOE DICKENS *in the chest.*)

JOE DICKENS: Fuckin' bitch. (*He falls dead.*)

BRYANT: No!

MELINDA: I'm...I'm sorry. (*She runs away.*)

BRYANT: Get up. Get up. I didn't mean it. I didn't mean
it! Get up. Please. Oh god, oh god, oh god.
   I'm sorry, Mommy.

(*Lights fade on* BRYANT *holding* JOE DICKENS' *dead body.*)

INTERLUDE:
JUSTICE PART THREE

(*As the next voice-over happens, we see news articles and
magazine covers depicting the arrest of Captain Justice,
closing on a image of* JASON *on the cover of* Time *magazine
with the heading "Who will protect us now?"*)

JUDGE: (*V O*) Jason Price A K A Captain Justice,
you seem to be a remorseless man in these crimes.
You openly admit that you hunted down these
individuals and then killed them in cold blood.
You used every bit of your government training
and enhanced abilities to not only murder, but torture,
maim, and cruelly batter these two individuals. As a
man of the state—a soldier that our blessed United

States of America has entrusted as a protector, you are held to a higher jurisdiction than most—one who cannot, should not, and will never again be subject to your passions, the court hereby orders you to serve two life sentences in solitary, back to back, one for each of your victims. You will serve this sentence at The Steel City Correctional Facility in Nevada which is specially equipped to deal with inmates with your unique abilities. May you never see the light of day again and may God have mercy on your wretched soul.

(Projection: "To be continued...")

END OF PART ONE

PART TWO

SCENE IV

(Projection: "Chapter Four: Steel City")

(Projection: "At a Classified Location")

(WARDEN's office. The present)

(WARDEN addressing a new officer.)

WARDEN: I know you've probably heard rumors about this facility—this lovely strip of land in the middle of nowhere. But I assure you we're housing no space aliens, stargates, or wreckage from any crash landings. There is no conspiracy happening here and I have zero interest in experimenting on any of our subjects. This is simply a prison. A prison housing the most dangerous criminals on this planet. Prisoners who, as you know, are enhanced. This is Steel City—the only penitentiary of its kind. If you wish to work here, we could use a man of your expertise. Our boys up in Chicago speak very highly of you, Mister Wallace. You've garnered quite a reputation in being a very stern, but fair correctional officer.

MALCOLM: Thank you. I think I'll be quite happy here. And, please, call me Malcolm.

WARDEN: Well, Malcolm, as you know, we have recently picked up some celebrity clientele. Captain Justice. He's being held in solitary where we'd like to assign you.

MALCOLM: Solitary?

WARDEN: Yes.

MALCOLM: I don't know, Warden. I'm more used to working with Gen-Pop. Solitary honestly kinda bores me.

WARDEN: But the opportunity to work with—

MALCOLM: Closed doors and empty hallways? Doesn't sound very active.

WARDEN: The truth is, Malcolm, we've been having some issues with the guards in C-block. They feel some guilt over housing one of these so-called heroes. We've had five men walk and several have even joined the protests outside. I need someone I can trust running that sector.

MALCOLM: How do you know I'm not a sympathizer?

WARDEN: We've seen your records from M C C-Chicago, we know you aren't some bleeding heart. And you don't share any particular affinities for Captain Justice, now do you?

MALCOLM: I assure you, Warden—Captain Justice is only a man to me—nothing more.

(Fade to...)

*(*DAMON *and* LUKAS *in their cells.)*

DAMON: Yo, Luke, we should sneak over to Solitary and see if we can get a spy on Captain J.

LUKAS: You fucking crazy, dawg?

DAMON: What?

LUKAS: Sneak over to Solitary? We can't even sneak out of our own fuckin' cells unless them hacks let us. Shit, son, you think we Houdini or some shit all of a sudden?

DAMON: I'm just playin'.

LUKAS: Well, play like you got some sense, dawg. That shit is ignorant.

DAMON: Come on, Luke. What? You ain't excited he's here. It's Captain Justice, hero to the world and what not.

LUKAS: Who cares?

DAMON: What do you mean who cares? You care. You useta collect newspaper articles about him, remember? Dressed up like him during Halloween. You even tried to get me to be Liberty Lady that one year, but I was like—no way, I don't look good in fishnets.

LUKAS: That was a long time ago, D.

DAMON: Yo, where is your sense of adventure? Where's the Luke that useta be fearless and all that? The guy who once ate fifty hot-dogs on a dare. A dare. You smelled like a fucking frank for a month. That shit was nasty. What happened to that guy, huh?

LUKAS: He got locked up.

DAMON: Yo, man, I'm sorry about that.

LUKAS: Save it.

DAMON: I wonder how Camille's doing. You think she misses us? I mean, I'd miss us. We two very miss-worthy dudes. She has to miss us, right?

LUKAS: Naw.

DAMON: What do you mean "Naw"?

LUKAS: I mean—I don't think she misses shit.

DAMON: How you gonna say that? She's my sister. My own flesh and blood. She has to miss me— it's like her job and shit.

LUKAS: Right.

DAMON: Why you being so negative?

LUKAS: I ain't being negative.

DAMON: What? You think this is instilling me with a bunch of confidence over our situation? You think this is supportive words.

LUKAS: Yo, you asked my opinion, I gave it.

DAMON: Your opinion was suppose to be "yes".

LUKAS: Look, dawg, if she misses you so bad—how come she never writes? Come visit and what not? How come we ain't never heard from her since we got here?

DAMON: Address.

LUKAS: What?

DAMON: She must have lost the address. She doesn't know where to get in contact. This is a very far away location. We're in the middle of nowhere, Nevada.

LUKAS: Whatever, dawg.

DAMON: Yo, why are you hatin'? I'm just talking about my family.

LUKAS: I'm not hatin'.

DAMON: What you doin' then?

LUKAS: D, your sister ain't talking to you cause you in jail. You in jail cause you shot up a cop—a cop who happened to be her boyfriend. Do you see a connection? Do you see why she might not think fondly on you about this?

DAMON: It was an accident.

LUKAS: Whatever, dawg. I'm going to sleep.

DAMON: You were there—you know it was an accident.

LUKAS: Accidents are what happens when white folks shoot up somebody. They call it "involuntary manslaughter" or "unintentional homicide" or some

shit fancy term meaning they ain't going to jail.
Folks like us, however—we should just be happy
we ain't hangin' by our necks.

DAMON: You bleak, dawg.

LUKAS: Yeah, I'm a bleak motherfucker. I'm a stormy
fuckin' cloud. Getting thrown in the pen does that to
a motherfucka.

DAMON: Luke?

LUKAS: Look, D, I don't give a shit no more. About
Captain Justice, Liberty Lady, all them supers—they
can go fuck themselves for all I care. Do you know what
I want to see? What I really want to see? I wanna see
my ratty ass apartment again. Fuckin' Marcus and King
acting like fools on the corner. I wanna see your bitch
ass sister again—our boys at the bodega—fuckin'
Dominican flags hangin' from windows and what not.
I wanna see Bushwick. I wanna see home. But ya know
what? That ain't gonna happen.

   The truth is there's no use to be worrying about
Camille or addresses or who misses who. Look at
us—look where we at. Everything we are, will be,
is this. Nothin. We just a whole lotta wasted nothin'.
And that, D, ain't gonna change by meeting Captain J.

(Meanwhile in Solitary...)

(Lights come up on JASON.*)*

(A figure emerges. She giggles.)

JASON: Helen?

HELEN: Look at you. Look at my mighty mighty
superhero. What have they done to you, my dear?

JASON: No. You're not here.

HELEN: That's very astute of you. You're right. I'm not
here. I'm a figment. An image. An illusive entity created
in your mind solely to torment you. To push your

buttons. To keep you company in this dark dark dank place. Is it working?

JASON: I miss you.

HELEN: Don't fall for it yet, baby. You start talking to me now, then you're really crazy. I mean, crazy crazy. I'm talking poop in your hand and rub it all over your face crazy.

JASON: You're dead. They killed you. You're not here.

HELEN: Shhhh.
   How are you, baby? How are you doing?

JASON: I'm—

HELEN: Peep, peep, peep!
   Just think it. I'm in your head. I'll hear.
   Good. You're good? Liar.
   You aren't good, baby. You're in trouble. Cause let's be honest, sitting here—hanging out in this never-ending hole of torment—that's very far from good.

JASON: They killed you.

HELEN: I'm sorry, baby. I'm sorry. But you got your revenge, didn't you? You got them good. For me.

JASON: I'd do it again. If I could, I would.

HELEN: Now, there you are. There's my champion. *(She exits.)*

JASON: Helen! *(Dressed in rags, he sits quietly in his prison cell.)*

(The small opaque window to his cell door opens.)

MALCOLM: Psst. Psst. Over here.

(JASON looks.)

MALCOLM: Hey there, old friend. How ya doing?

JASON: Are you God?

MALCOLM: No, Jason, I'm not God. But it's flattering that you'd mistaken me for him.

JASON: What do you want?

MALCOLM: Thought you could use the company.

JASON: Go away! If you're here, she won't come back.

MALCOLM: Who?

JASON: Helen. My figment. My Helen.

MALCOLM: What the hell did they do to you?

JASON: I want her to come back. Go away!

MALCOLM: Jason, she's dead.

JASON: Shhh. She knows that. She's vastly intelligent.

MALCOLM: Jason, you need to get out of here. This place is driving you insane.

JASON: NO! I have to be here. I need to be punished. It's the American way. Punish the weak.

MALCOLM: No, Jason, you're a hero.

JASON: Not anymore, not anymore.

MALCOLM: How many times have you saved this world—a few hundred? Jason, if it weren't for you— some mad scientist or radioactive monster would have surely leveled this fucking country by now. And what— that don't mean shit? They still lock you up for giving a coupla scumbags a dirt nap? That's fucked up. Entirely fucked up.

JASON: I hunted them down like dogs. They had to punish me.

MALCOLM: Still ever the idealist, I see.

JASON: I'm a bad guy now. A supervillian.

MALCOLM: Jason, anyone would have done the same.

JASON: You are God, aren't you? You have God's voice.

MALCOLM: No, Jason. You are.

JASON: I like you.

MALCOLM: We're going to make you whole again, my friend. And we'll fight our way out of here together—the way it was intended.

(Meanwhile in the cafeteria...)

(BRYANT and DAMON sitting alone at a cafeteria table. BRYANT stares at DAMON as he eats.)

(DAMON gets anxious about being watched.)

DAMON: Yo, dawg, can I help you with something?

BRYANT: I like your hair.

DAMON: My hair?

BRYANT: It's curly.

DAMON: Um, you ain't saying that cause you gonna like tie me up and cut it off my scalp or nothin', right? You ain't crazy like that, right?

BRYANT: I useta wear a wig like that when men beat me up. I wore that one when they wanted me to look like a Mexican.

DAMON: Say what?

BRYANT: Or a Jew. Or a Black girl.

DAMON: Yo, that's fucked up. Why you telling me this?

BRYANT: They love to hit. I make a good punching bag.

DAMON: What?

BRYANT: You know—a punching bag. A bag that people hit. They paid me to do it.

DAMON: Whoa, you let guys hit you, dawg?

BRYANT: Uh-huh.

DAMON: Yo, that's fucked up. You like one fucked up dude, you know that?

BRYANT: It doesn't hurt.

DAMON: It musta hurt something. You don't seem to think so good, bro.

BRYANT: I've always been like this.

DAMON: No, man, you probably think you always been like this, but I bet you useta be like a rocket scientist or some shit, but now you're all fuckin' retarded cause of getting smacked around so much.

BRYANT: I'm not a scientist.

DAMON: Not anymore, you're not.

BRYANT: I never was—

DAMON: You got amnesia or something.

BRYANT: What's that?

DAMON: It's like a disease, makes you like all forgetful and shit. Like Ronald Reagan or George Bush. Fuckin' stupid.

BRYANT: You're funny.

DAMON: Okay, man, no need to get all touchy touchy.

BRYANT: No, I can't get hurt. I'm special.

DAMON: Yeah, I can tell you're special, bro. Like special bus.

BRYANT: No. I can't feel hurt.

DAMON: Yo, dawg, everyone feels hurt.

BRYANT: Not me.

DAMON: Sure.

BRYANT: Look. See. *(He picks up a spork and jabs himself in the leg. He lets out a big scream.)* Aaaah!

DAMON: What the fuck, dude? What the fuck?

BRYANT: It hurts.

DAMON: No, shit, it hurts—you fucking jabbed a fucking spork in your leg, *pendejo.* That's fucking crazy, man. That's fucking...no, don't pull it out. We don't need you squirtin' blood everywhere making the ground all slip and slide.

BRYANT: But it hurts.

DAMON: Just keep your hand on it, bro. Yeah, man, you can't just fucking sit here and bleed to death. That'd be like really fucking gross.

BRYANT: You're helping me?

DAMON: HEY, GUARD! GUARD!

(Fade to...)

(Location: CELL BLOCK B.)

(MAELSTROM sneaking away to have a cigarette. As he lights it, ANDY appears from the shadows and grabs him.)

(ANDY holds a shank pointed a MALCOLM's neck.)

ANDY: Hey there, Malcolm? Remember me?

MAELSTROM: Who?

ANDY: Shhhh...

MAELSTROM: What do you want?

ANDY: No, no, no, no...I ask the questions. Not you. Me, I'm the one who gets to do the asking. Do you understand?

MAELSTROM: Sure.

ANDY: So shut the fuck up before I decide to pierce your goddamn trachea! Good, good—you know how to listen. You're finally listening—you've grown up to be quite the gentlemen, Malcolm. Congratulations. Congratu-fucking-lations. You almost seem human.

MAELSTROM: I'm glad that impresses you.

ANDY: Hehe, you think you're cute, don't you? Shut up. I didn't believe it was you at first, Mal. I thought— I must be going crazy. Malcolm Wallace? Here? No way. That rich little spoiled brat—that fucking entitled piece of trash—that goddamn lunatic, there's no way he'd be here. Not in Steel City—not as a C O. But there you were...fucking standing there as a fucking guard all happy in your stupid little uniform acting as superior as always. Acting all high and mighty. Acting like a fucking dickhead. I'm here—stuck in this fucking hell-hole because of your boyfriend—fucking cleaning up people's shit, getting fucking beat up, whored out, ripped to shreds and there you are—pretending to be a guard. Pretending like you give a shit.

MAELSTROM: Andy?

ANDY: Shut up! Shut the fuck up. I should have known you would have appeared here—especially since "big blue" got thrown in jail. Pulled some strings, created a new identity—it was only a matter of time before all you fucking supers were going to rally together and free his ass. Well, not this time, not without me. Not without saving the Hooded Menace, first! You got me? So you're gonna fucking save me, Malcolm. It's my turn to get some fucking saving.

 This is your fault I'm here. This is your fucking fault I'm trapped in this cesspool.

MAELSTROM: Andy, I wasn't the one who brought you in.

ANDY: NO, but you were the one who made me.

MAELSTROM: Andy—

ANDY: I didn't believe I'd ever see you again. You look good. You grew up. I tried—I tried to get your attention, Mal, for so long. Grew up, became strong, made myself into someone who would be taken seriously.

MAELSTROM: Andy, I suggest you let me go.

ANDY: Shut up. SHUT THE FUCK UP!
   Remember when you fucked me, Mal? Do you remember when you stole my virginity and then threw me away like some used condom? Do you remember that? ANSWER ME!

MAELSTROM: I didn't steal—

ANDY: SHUT UP! That's not what I asked. I asked a yes/no question requiring a yes/no answer. Do you remember?

MAELSTROM: Yes.

ANDY: Well, Mal, it's time for some fucking payback.

MAELSTROM: You're making a mistake there, friend. A really big mistake.

ANDY: Take off your pants.

MAELSTROM: Andy.

ANDY: Take off your fucking pants. Now.

(Beat)

MAELSTROM: I'm sorry.

ANDY: You're what?

MAELSTROM: I said I'm sorry, Andy. I'm sorry.

ANDY: Well, it's a little too late for that, don't you think? It's a little too late to be apologizing for hurting my feelings.

MAELSTROM: I'm not apologizing for that.

ANDY: Then what are you—

(MAELSTROM *grabs* ANDY'*s arm and reverses the hold.*)

MAELSTROM: I was apologizing for this.

(MAELSTROM *raises the blade to stab* ANDY. LUKAS *rushes in and pushes* MAELSTROM *off.*)

LUKAS: Yo, what the fuck you doin', dawg?

MAELSTROM: Mind your own business, friend.

LUKAS: I'm not trying to be a hero or nuthin'. But if you kill that guy...I'm the one who has to clean that shit up.

(MAELSTROM *throws the shank onto the ground and exits.*)

LUKAS: What was up with you and that hack?

ANDY: We're old friends.

LUKAS: Friends? Yo, I gots friends. Friends don't try to run kitchen items through your gut.

ANDY: My friends do.

LUKAS: Well, perhaps you need to re-evaluate your Christmas card list, bro.

ANDY: What are you in here for? Mass murder? World domination? What's your story, stranger?

LUKAS: My name's Lukas and I ain't got one. I'm what they call an innocent man.

ANDY: Right. Aren't we all?

LUKAS: Yeah, but, see, I'm actually innocent. I ain't done shit.
  So what's your story?

ANDY: My story? Once upon a time ago I was the Hooded Menace.

LUKAS: Say what?

ANDY: You heard of me?

LUKAS: You the Hooded Menace? You? Your scrawny ass was Captain J's Big Bad? You?

ANDY: Is that surprising?

LUKAS: Yo dawg, no offence, but you ain't exactly all that scarfaced.

ANDY: Sorry to disappoint.

LUKAS: No, man, I'm just sayin'—I just thought you'd be a bit more scary. The way they painted you in the news—

ANDY: You trust everything you read? The job of journalists is to sell papers, not report the truth.

LUKAS: Yo, man, is it true that you once got beat up by Captain J and Maelstrom because you talked too much?

ANDY: That was The Mole, not me.

LUKAS: Yo, that shit was funny

ANDY: Is it?

LUKAS: Yeah, man. Fuckin' stupid ass shit.

ANDY: Do you know what happened to The Mole?

LUKAS: Naw.

ANDY: He was one of the first to be incarcerated here, Lukas. And do you know what happened to him? This is great—this is funny. The guards locked him up in solitary.
    And because they knew he had powers like a mole, they left him alone. Completely alone. They were so scared to be near him that they refused food and water assuming his powers would keep him alive. For months.

LUKAS: What happened?

ANDY: He died here, Lukas.

They didn't report that, now did they? That wouldn't have sold papers. Is that funny? Is that stupid ass shit?

LUKAS: Yo, dawg, you dark.

ANDY: We live in a world of lies, Lukas. Listen to those sheep outside. You hear them?

LUKAS: Naw.

ANDY: I do. From miles and miles around—they're all fighting for one man. One man. Captain Justice. People are outraged.

LUKAS: Of course they are. He's a super.

ANDY: He's a criminal, just like you and me.

He killed someone. Someones. In cold blood and people are outraged that he has to make amends for those murders. What makes him different, Lukas? What?

LUKAS: I don't know.

ANDY: He has the news on his side. Do you know why I fought him for so long? All these years?

LUKAS: Cause you evil?

ANDY: I was there to keep him honest—to keep him from realizing his full potential. No man should have the power he has—the power any of those supers have. If it weren't for people like me, how long would it be before they figure it's easier to rule us than to protect us?

And now, we have the most powerful of them sitting in a cage next to ours. What's gonna happen when he grows tired of wearing the mask of humanity?

I'm scared of him, Lukas, as we all should be.

(*Fade to...*)

(JASON *in his cell. Across from him sits* HELEN.)

JASON: You don't know what it was like for me, Helen. Having this much power. It's like God kissing every muscle—every joint—every particle which makes up me. I feel nothing of this world. No pain equals no pleasure—both sensations connected by a thread so fine that sometimes you can't tell where one ends and the other begins. All I have is power—this constant throbbing vibration within—a power that I feel eating away at me—a power changing me—evolving me— turning me into something beyond this mortal coil.

They didn't make a hero when they turned me into Captain Justice, Helen. They just recreated the Atom Bomb into the from of man.

I like being here—being with you. Out there, I walk among eggshells. I tiptoe between dolls made of rice paper careful not to breath too hard, touch too abrasively, embrace anything—anyone—with passion. For if I'm not careful, I'll blow away humanity itself as if it were a Buddhist sand painting.

But here—here the world is safe from me.

And I get to be with you.

(Fade to...)

(Steel City rec center.)

MALCOLM: Hey there, Liberty. It's been a long time since I've seen you in civies.

LIBERTY LADY: Same here.

MALCOLM: Care for a drink?

LIBERTY LADY: I'm not in uniform, am I?

(MALCOLM *pulls out a flask and throws it to* LIBERTY LADY. *She catches it with ease.*)

LIBERTY LADY: Whiskey?

MALCOLM: Johnny Blue. You know I only drink the best.

LIBERTY LADY: You can take the boy out of the country club...

MALCOLM: I see you brought it.

LIBERTY LADY: Yes. I said I would.

MALCOLM: Hand it here.

LIBERTY LADY: I don't know, Mal.

MALCOLM: What do you mean you don't know?

LIBERTY LADY: As in I'm not sure—not one hundred percent confident in the situation.

MALCOLM: Become confident.

LIBERTY LADY: Jason chose to be locked up, Mal. He chose to be here. I don't know if what we're doing is right.

MALCOLM: And letting him rot is?

LIBERTY LADY: You haven't been out on the streets, Malcolm. Things have changed out there ever since Jason killed those two guys. I hear them, Mal. I hear the fear in their voices when they see me. They used to cheer for us—they used to look at us as hope. But the longer we're here, the longer we fight for them—they're starting to see us as the enemy.

MALCOLM: I'm less concerned about them at this point, Liberty. Where my concern lies is in Jason.

LIBERTY LADY: Maybe letting him stay here is the right thing to do.

MALCOLM: I know the pain he's going through. It's the same pain I felt when my father was killed—the same pain that made me decide to become Maelstrom. He now understands me. He knows what it mean to take this job personally.

LIBERTY LADY: He killed people, Mal.

MALCOLM: In a war, we sometimes have to do questionable things to achieve our objective.

(Silence)

LIBERTY LADY: He's broken the law, Mal. Publicly. Whether you want to accept this or not, he deserves to be here.
  I'm sorry, Mal—I can't give it to you.

MALCOLM: You came all this way to tell me no?

LIBERTY LADY: Well, it's looking like I came all this way to stop you.

MALCOLM: You know I told him years ago you were nothing more than a P.R. stunt—that you'd never evolve into anything more than just his lame teenage sidekick. I guess I was right. Without him, you think for shit.

LIBERTY LADY: Why? Because I have an opinion, that makes me stupid?

MALCOLM: No. It's because you actually thought that was scotch, that's what makes you stupid.

(LIBERTY LADY *stands up and punches* MALCOLM. *He's not affected.)*

(LIBERTY LADY *passes out.)*

MALCOLM: See ya round the crime lab, love.

(Fade to...)

DAMON: You going to be okay?

BRYANT: I hurt myself.

DAMON: Yeah, I saw that. Why the fuck did you do that, dawg?

BRYANT: I can't feel hurt.

DAMON: Well, apparently, you do.

BRYANT: No, I can't.

DAMON: Then what's this?

(DAMON *pokes* BRYANT*'s wound.*)

BRYANT: Ow!

DAMON: That is the sound of you being wrong, bro. You are definitely feeling the pain.

BRYANT: I don't understand.

DAMON: Yes, I'm sure that is a state of being you're very used to by now, huh?

(LUKAS *enters.*)

LUKAS: Hey.

DAMON: Hey Luke.

LUKAS: Yo, who's this guy?

DAMON: This guy? He's a friend.

BRYANT: I'm a friend.

LUKAS: What the hell happened to his leg?

DAMON: He stabbed himself.

BRYANT: I stabbed myself.

DAMON: It was insane, dawg. It was like one of them Evil Dead movies, yo. Blood was spurting everywhere.

BRYANT: It was everywhere.

LUKAS: Does your boy here have to repeat everything you say?

DAMON: No.

BRYANT: No.

LUKAS: What's your power, *pendejo*? You repeat shit? You like the repeater?

DAMON: Yo, dawg, don't be rude. He's a good guy.

BRYANT: I can't get hurt.

LUKAS: You can't get what?

DAMON: Yeah, he's been saying that alot. Obviously that ain't the case.

BRYANT: You can hit me if you want.

DAMON: I don't know what makes him think he can't get—

(LUKAS *punches* BRYANT *in the stomach hard.* BRYANT *doesn't feel it.*)

DAMON: Yo, why'd you do that?

LUKAS: He said I could.

DAMON: Yo, man, you coulda hurt him.

LUKAS: Obviously, I didn't though. Look at him.

BRYANT: I told you.

(LUKAS *punches* BRYANT *over and over. No pain registers.*)

LUKAS: Holy fuck, this shit is da bomb, yo.

DAMON: Stop that.

BRYANT: It's okay, I don't mind.

DAMON: No, man. You can't let people do this to you. It's not right.

BRYANT: But I'm okay.

DAMON: It don't matter.

LUKAS: Yo, chill out. We just fuckin' around. You should take a swing—relieve some tension.

BRYANT: You can if you want.

DAMON: Naw, man.

LUKAS: Come on, D, don't be a pussy. Hit the motherfucka.

DAMON: No.

BRYANT: You can hit me in the face if you want?

DAMON: No.

LUKAS: Aw, man, can I hit him in the face?

DAMON: No.

BRYANT: If you want, I'll let you.

DAMON: No.

LUKAS: Please?

DAMON: No.

BRYANT: It won't hurt.

DAMON: No.

LUKAS: Listen to him.

DAMON: Alright, fine!

(DAMON *slugs* BRYANT *in the face.* BRYANT *feels it.*)

BRYANT: OW!

DAMON: Shit, I'm sorry. I didn't mean—

BRYANT: You hurt me!

DAMON: I'm sorry!

LUKAS: Yo, hold up.

(LUKAS *pulls* DAMON *away from* BRYANT.)

DAMON: What are you doing?

LUKAS: I got an idea.

DAMON: You got a what?

LUKAS: An idea, *pendejo.* An idea.
  Hit the wall.

DAMON: What?

LUKAS: Hit the motherfuckin' wall. Break it, then we can get our asses outta here.

DAMON: I'm not going to hit the wall. I'll break my hand.

LUKAS: No, you won't. Check it—you gots superstrength, bro. That's how you hurt him. Look at you. Look at me. I hit that big retarded motherfucker, nothin happens. You hit him and he's cryin' like a lil' bitch. You gots superstrength.

BRYANT: You're strong? My mom was strong.

DAMON: I don't feel strong.

LUKAS: Do it, man. Get our asses out of here. Get us home.

DAMON: I have superstrength?

LUKAS: You gots superstrength.

BRYANT: Wow.

DAMON: Okay.

LUKAS: Alright. You hear that, *pendejo*? We gonna get outta here!

(DAMON *rears his fist back.*)

LUKAS: Aw, man, this is gonna be awesome.

(DAMON *runs into the wall. Nothing happens, except* DAMON *falls to the ground in excruciating pain.*)

DAMON: OW!!!

LUKAS: Yo, man, you didn't break the wall.

DAMON: I know! I think I broke my face.

LUKAS: Yo, man, you ain't strong.

DAMON: I know.

LUKAS: Then how?

BRYANT: Maybe God made you special in a different way.

DAMON: What do you mean?

BRYANT: Maybe you don't got power. Maybe you take it away.

DAMON: Wait. Yeah, maybe that's it.

LUKAS: What? The hell are you two smokin'?

BRYANT: You're a super.

LUKAS: Bullshit.

DAMON: You know, I always knew I was destined for greatness.

LUKAS: You destined to do another ten to twenty. Shit, son, that ain't so great.

DAMON: I'm serious, Luke. Maybe Bryant's right. I'm a power-sucker.

LUKAS: Yeah, you definitely suckin' somethin'.

DAMON: That why I can hurt him and you can't. I have the power to even the playing field. That's pretty awesome.

LUKAS: Yo, dawg, that ain't awesome. That ain't even a power. That's like an anti-power.

DAMON: It's still pretty cool.

LUKAS: It's not cool. You're like a fuckin' off-switch.

DAMON: Do I sense jealousy?

LUKAS: I ain't jealous.

DAMON: I think maybe you are.

LUKAS: I think I maybe kicking your ass you keep calling me jealous.

DAMON: Yo, dawg, there ain't no reason for all that.

(Fade to...)

(JASON *in his cell*)

(A spotlight comes up on the CAPTAIN JUSTICE *shield that lies directly in front of* JASON.*)*

JASON: It's not real, it's not real, it's not real.

HELEN: Take it.

JASON: No, no, no. Not real.

HELEN: Take it.

JASON: Don't make me do this. Please.

(The window of the cell door slides open.)

MALCOLM: Hey, Cap. Like your present?

JASON: The shield? The shield's not real.

MALCOLM: Take it. Try it on.

JASON: Too dangerous. Too dangerous to hold it.

MALCOLM: You're a hero, Jason. It's time to remember that. Take it.

JASON: No, I can't. I can't.

MALCOLM: Jason, listen to me. The world needs you again. I need you.

JASON: No. I failed. She died. She died.

MALCOLM: You miss her, don't you?

JASON: Helen.

HELEN: I love you, baby.

MALCOLM: You should miss her. Evil men took her life, Jason—ripped her away from you—stole the one person that mattered most.

JASON: It's all my fault. I should have been there. I should have been with her.

MALCOLM: Yes, you should have. But where were you?

JASON: I'm so sorry. I'm so so sorry. Please forgive me. Please, please, please.

MALCOLM: You have to take this shield, Jason. You have to embrace your true destiny.

HELEN: Save me.

MALCOLM: Be a hero, Jason, but this time be a real hero.

JASON: A real hero?

MALCOLM: What do you say, old friend? Wanna save the world?

(Fade to...)

*(*BRYANT, LUKAS, *and* DAMON*)*

(An ALARM goes off.)

DAMON: Yo, what the fuck is that?

LUKAS: A lockdown maybe?

BRYANT: It's loud.

DAMON: Do you think we're in trouble?

LUKAS: I'm sure it's nothing.

DAMON: Nothing? What do you think that alarm is? You think that's a good omen? That's the what— the happy alarm? The "it's all good" alert.

*(*ANDY *suddenly runs onto stage. He's bloodied and hurt. He collapses in front of* DAMON, LUKAS, *and* BRYANT. *The alarm abruptly goes off.)*

ANDY: Lukas! Help.

LUKAS: Andy?

DAMON: I told you we were in trouble.

ANDY: Lukas, you gotta hide me.

BRYANT: Who's he?

LUKAS: Yo, dawg, what's wrong with you?

ANDY: Justice. He's lost it. He's really fuckin' lost it. He's going crazy, Luke. He's going fuckin' crazy.

DAMON: Yo, Luke, who is this guy?

ANDY: You gotta hide me.

LUKAS: We gotta get you to the infirmary, that's what we gotta do. You don't look so good, bro.

ANDY: No. No time.

DAMON: Luke, why's your boy there all fucked up?

LUKAS: I don't know. Help me with him, will ya?

(JASON *and* MALCOLM *enter.*)

JASON: Stand back, citizens. Captain Justice is here.

LUKAS: Holy fuck.

DAMON: Holy fuck is right.

MAELSTROM: Look, Jason, it's your arch-nemesis— The Hooded Menace.

CAPTAIN JUSTICE: Menace, even without my costume, I can still show your goons a true American welcome. Surrender yourself.

ANDY: Help me.

LUKAS: Yo, J, how ya doin', bro? Can we like talk about this?

CAPTAIN JUSTICE: The time for talk is over.

(JASON *smacks* LUKAS *to the ground.*)

LUKAS: *(To* BRYANT*)* Do something!

(BRYANT *steps in the way between* JASON *and the boys.* JASON *hits* BRYANT *twice with his shield. The impact rattles everyone to the ground.*)

(As they struggle, DAMON *grabs* JASON *and depowers him for a second, giving* BRYANT *the advantage.)*

(However, JASON *pushes* BRYANT *into* DAMON *which turns* BRYANT *vulnerable.* JASON *takes out* BRYANT.*)*

*(*LUKAS *and* DAMON *try to charge into the fight, but with superspeed,* JASON *takes his shield and knocks the boys to the ground.)*

JASON: Well, Menace, I guess you once again underestimated the power of truth, justice and the American Way.

ANDY: What are you going to do to me, Cap? Throw me deeper into prison? I'm already here in jail.

JASON: No, Menace. Not this time. This time it ends for good.

*(*JASON *prepares to throw the shield through* ANDY, *however* LIBERTY LADY *runs through with superspeed and grabs his weapon and tosses it at him.* JASON *falls.)*

LIBERTY LADY: Captain, stop! Don't do it.

JASON: Liberty? What are you doing here?

LIBERTY LADY: You can't do this, Jason. I won't let you.

MAELSTROM: Mind your own business, Liberty.

LIBERTY LADY: Cap, please, you gotta stop.

JASON: Move out of my way, Liberty. This is an order.

LIBERTY LADY: I'm not your sidekick anymore, Cap. Stand down. I order you.

JASON: You'd protect him?

LIBERTY LADY: To protect you...yes.

*(*JASON *lowers his shield.)*

JASON: Liberty...

MAELSTROM: No.

JASON: What am I doing?

(Suddenly, MAELSTROM *goes for the kill on* ANDY. JASON *stops him.)*

JASON: No, Malcolm. It's going to be okay. Liberty's here.

MAELSTROM: No, Jason, it's not. I'm sorry, but I have to do this. For you. For America.

*(*MAELSTROM *pulls a device and presses it. A wave of sound rattles* JASON *and* LIBERTY LADY'*s ears. They crumble in pain.)*

(Seeing this, DAMON, LUKAS, *and* BRYANT *try to help them.* MAELSTROM *beats down the boys heavily, but* BRYANT *manages to stop the sound wave.)*

*(*LIBERTY LADY *rushes to fight* MAELSTROM, *but he's taken the shield and is able to defend himself easily from* LIBERTY LADY'*s attack.)*

(Suddenly, DAMON, LUKAS, *and* BRYANT *jump into the fight to stop* MAELSTROM. *And though they take an early advantage,* MAELSTROM *is able to take them down.)*

(After all his opponents are down, MAELSTROM *grabs* ANDY *by the foot and drags him into the center of the room. He pulls out a knife and places it on* ANDY'*s neck.)*

JASON: Malcolm, stop!

MAELSTROM: Have you learned nothing?

JASON: Liberty's right. We can't do this.

MAELSTROM: I killed Helen.

JASON: What?

MAELSTROM: I killed Helen. I let her die.

JASON: You're lying!

MAELSTROM: I'm a bad guy, Jason. I'm the vilest of the vile. I am humanity and humanity is corrupt. I ask you, Captain Justice, what is your verdict? How would you punish a man like me? A man who killed your wife...

(JASON *picks up his shield and looks at it.*)

(HELEN *enters.*)

HELEN: Save me, Jason. Do it. Be my champion.

MAELSTROM: What do you say, Captain? What is your judgement?

HELEN: Be my hero.

JASON: I miss you, Helen.

HELEN: I miss you too, baby.

(JASON *looks to* MAELSTROM)

JASON: But I'm not a God. I'm just a man. *(He steps towards his old friend.)* Or at least I'm trying to be one.

(JASON *gives his hand to* ANDY *who stands up with him. As he does, the rest of the cast rise from the ground surrounding* MAELSTROM *as a united front.*)

MAELSTROM: *(Defeated)* Then we truly are lost. *(He lowers his weapon.)*

JASON: Go home, Mal.

(MAELSTROM *closes his knife and hands it to* JASON.)

(MAELSTROM *quietly exits.*)

(HELEN *gives* JASON *a smile and disappears from stage.*)

(LIBERTY LADY *approaches.*)

LIBERTY LADY: Hey, Cap. You gonna be alright?

JASON: No, Liberty. I don't think I will.

(LIBERTY LADY *goes to comfort* JASON *as* DAMON *approaches.*)

DAMON: Yo, Justice... *(He places his hand on* JASON's *shoulder.)* Could I get your autograph?

LUKAS: D!

DAMON: Maybe later.

*(*JASON *smiles.)*

LIBERTY LADY: Liberty and Justice for all.

(Lights go to black.)

(Projection: "The End")

END OF PLAY